# THE TRAUMA MAP

## FIVE STEPS TO RECONNECT WITH YOURSELF

By Dr. Karol Darsa

Publisher's Cataloging-in-Publication data Darsa, Karol

Editor: Corrine Casanova
Cover design: Lilah Higgins
Interior design: Andrea Reider

ISBN: 978-1-7355980-0-0 (paperback)
ISBN: 978-2-7355980-1-7 (ebook)

1. Psychology
2. Post-Traumatic Stress Disorder (PTSD)
3. Self-Help

First Edition


**Disclaimer:** Information in this book is meant to supplement therapy, not replace it. Names and identifying details of clients have been changed to protect their identities.

## Advance Praise

"Dr. Darsa's book is just the salve and balm a trauma survivor needs. Darsa clearly explains how unprocessed trauma can hold us hostage and provides a practical guide to a series of simple steps anyone can take to unshackle themselves from its bonds.

For anyone who has ever suffered from or continues to struggle in the wake of a traumatic break — this book provides readers with basic and easy tools to heal, and not just survive, but thrive.

Darsa's lucid prose nourishes, empowers and heals. I know whomever reads it will feel enlightened, uplifted and provided with the means to finally achieve much needed and much deserved peace."

— Amy Ziering
Two-time Emmy® Award winning and Academy Award® nominated documentary filmmaker

"As a healthcare provider for over 25 years, I was so impressed with *The Trauma Map*. It certainly took me back to my medical school years and made me realize that I too had PTSD. As a physician, I found many helpful directions and interventions to use with my patients. There are also great tools for those who have suffered from past events or experiences and are looking for help or guidance on how to deal with them. I am sure many people will benefit from this book, as I did myself."

— Aykut Bayrak, M.D.
Medical Director
Los Angeles IVF Clinic

"Dr. Karol Darsa, founder of the nationally renowned Reconnect Integrative Trauma Treatment Center is a true expert in the art and science of trauma work. In my opinion, *The Trauma Map - 5 Steps to Reconnect with Yourself* is a perfect blend of solid and helpful information, compelling case history, and practical wisdom for those suffering from the ill effects of trauma. This is a must-read for those who wish to understand and address adverse childhood experiences, as well as clinicians devoted to treating client trauma."

— Dr. Seth C. Kadish
Director of Group Therapy, PCH

"Dr. Karol has used her years of experience working with trauma patients to create this transformative self-help book. It is written with compassion and valuable insights, offering new techniques and hope for healing."

— Aileen Nobles
Intuitive/Theta/EFT/Hypnotherapy

"I truly believe that transforming trauma is the key to healing our planet. Dr. Darsa's life's work is reflected in *The Trauma Map*, which provides an accessible, step-by-step guide to reconnecting the body and mind after a traumatic impact. Dr. Darsa provides a beacon of hope for anyone moving through the shadows of traumatic impact."

— Dawn Delgado, LMFT, CEDS-S
EMDR Certified Trauma Therapist

"Trauma understood; treatment invaluable!

The title itself, *The Trauma Map* is exactly what this book presents for all those who are suffering from trauma or for professional therapists who work with clients who are longing to 'reconnect' with themselves.

Dr. Karol Darsa 'maps' out the ABCs of trauma, what it is, the symptoms, how it affects us, and especially how to work through it in a way that is easy to understand and process with compassion and empowerment. Her narrative is as though she is sitting with you, providing safety, knowledge, and skills to guide you through your journey in healing from your trauma.

As a therapist, I am thankful for this step-by-step 'map' that shares how to reconnect with one's self and move through trauma with all the careful considerations, a holistic (mind, body, spirit) approach, and strength-based exercises gained from 20 years of experiences with clients that cannot be taught in a graduate course. Thank you, Dr. Darsa, for sharing your professional insight and making your five steps of healing and self-care strategies accessible to all."

— Noranik Zadeyan, MPH, MA, LMHC
Master's in Public Health
Master's in Counseling

# Contents

*"Not until we are lost do we begin*
*to understand ourselves."*

—Henry David Thoreau

# Introduction

Most likely you've picked up this book because you, or a loved one, have experienced or are experiencing some type of traumatic situation or event. You may be wondering if it's possible to recover and heal from it. I am here to tell you, *yes,* healing and recovery from trauma are possible.

Some people are unsure if what they've been through is considered trauma and make comments such as:

- "I know my parents loved me, but they didn't spend any time with me—do I have trauma?"
- "I can't remember bad things happening to me as a kid, but I have nightmares every night—do I have trauma?"
- "I saw someone get in a bad car accident and I was first on the scene, but I don't think I have trauma because I don't feel anything at all."

I've dedicated my life and career to studying trauma and helping people just like you live well despite trauma. I am the founder and director of Reconnect Integrative Trauma Treatment Center in

Pacific Palisades, California. It's a one-of-a-kind treatment center that integrates all evidence-based, cutting-edge trauma treatment modalities under one roof. I created Reconnect because I saw that people were being treated for their symptoms, such as addiction, anxiety, and depression, instead of the root cause—trauma. Since 2012, my team and I have been successful in helping hundreds of people just like you overcome their traumatic pasts through our unique program. Our approach to trauma treatment is different: we use a gentle, body-based process to help heal and reconnect your mind and body.

Through the years, I've learned that you don't need to be a client in my treatment center to benefit from our unique five-step process for healing from trauma, which I'll be sharing with you. As these techniques have helped so many clients, including myself, I decided to write a book to help you as well. These five steps will help you reconnect with yourself and learn skills and tools to deal with your emotions and past trauma.

While this book isn't meant to replace therapy, it can supplement it. My goal is to give you tools that I have used over the years with clients who suffered from trauma. These tools will help you start the healing process and prepare you to continue the journey with a therapist if you choose. If you can't afford professional help or aren't interested in therapy, that's okay. This book will help you understand yourself and your past better and give you insight on how to deal with difficult feelings.

## Reconnect's Trauma Philosophy

Over my two decades of experience as a trauma psychologist, I have seen how trauma can create a disconnect. Trauma can make you feel disconnected from your body, heart, mind, loved ones, God, or spirituality—ultimately from who you truly are: your *whole self.* This book is based on the importance of *reconnecting with yourself first and foremost* as a way to heal from trauma.

I want to help you honor the most important relationship in this world: the one with yourself. I want to help you be whole, love yourself, love others, feel your life purpose, feel your body, and treat yourself in the best way. This is your birthright.

I want you to know that I am sorry for your pain. I am sorry for the trauma you experienced. The good news is that you can change your life for the better no matter how much pain you are feeling. You have to believe in this birthright, and you have to work at it, ideally with the support of someone else. Although you can never change the past, if you don't give up on yourself no matter what, you can have a loving life. If you commit to yourself, you can achieve inner peace. I know this to be true because I made this same commitment to myself.

To heal the past, you need to stay focused in the present. This means that your thoughts are not dispersed outside—you are in the here and now. You are not constantly thinking of the future or the past. You are not daydreaming about your lover or stuck in anger with your boss. Your thoughts are not racing—you are contained inside your body and are feeling content at this moment. I'll share how to do this here. Most people believe that trauma work means working through memories, but this is not the only way to move on from the past. The crucial component of healing from the past is being in the present moment and rebuilding your relationship with yourself.

Long-term, gradual healing takes time and commitment. Most likely, your trauma has been affecting you for a long time, and it may take some time to heal. You are worthy of that time and attention. You wouldn't abandon or rush a friend going through a healing process—you would give your friend all the time and support they need. You have the power to heal your own wounds with time and attention.

As you begin to accept how trauma has impacted you, you can become more compassionate with yourself and your emotional injuries. As Buddha stated, "You, yourself, as much as anybody in the entire universe, deserve your love and affection."

Most trauma survivors realize that they disconnected from themselves along the way, but they don't know how to reconnect with themselves. The following unique five-step process is what you'll need to heal from your trauma. And good news: I'll carefully share each of these steps with you within the pages of this book.

### Step 1: *Understand Trauma*

To understand yourself and to normalize your feelings, you need to know what trauma is. You've probably heard the phrase "Knowledge is power." Well, that holds true during this step. A lot of people minimize the impact of trauma. Until you understand the magnitude of the trauma, you can't start your healing process. Once you understand how trauma impacts both your physical and emotional well-being, things will make more sense.

### Step 2: *Reconnect to Your Mind*

During and after a traumatic event, your brain shuts down and makes it very difficult for you to think straight and make decisions. After you understand what trauma is and some of your reactions to it, you can start thinking clearly again so you can make decisions that benefit your well-being. Trauma clouds the way you think. This book focuses on mindfulness techniques to help you get clear-minded and reconnect with your mind.

### Step 3: *Reconnect to Your Body*

Learn how trauma may have disconnected you from your body through *dissociation*. That means rather than feeling strong emotions, you simply check out. Your body and mind are trying to protect you from overwhelming emotions, so your body numbs and shuts down. In this step, I share practical exercises and methods to help you reconnect to your body. In the early twenty-first century, the field of trauma treatment has clearly shown how important it is for trauma survivors to heal through the use of their bodies. Here, I offer practical and gentle exercises to help you make peace with your body again.

### Step 4: *Reconnect to Your Heart and Emotions*

You can't heal when you don't deal with negative feelings. You can't hide from your emotions. Trauma causes a lot of painful emotions that can become overwhelming. To deal with the painful feelings, you might have shut down your emotions. In this step, you will learn how to gradually make peace with your feelings without getting overwhelmed. I'll share ways to be gentle with your emotions relating to trauma and to release that sense of overwhelm.

### Step 5: *Reconnect to Spirituality, Community, Nature, and Family*

In this step, you will see how you may have isolated yourself due to trauma, recognize the dangers of isolation, and recognize the benefits of getting support from others. You will see how trauma has impacted your faith in a negative way. Faith means different things to different people. For you, it might be God, spirituality, or a connection with nature and the universe. It's time to restore that connection, and I'll show you how.

## You Are Not the Only One on This Journey

During Oprah Winfrey's 2020 Vision Tour, she interviewed Lady Gaga about how she deals with trauma and chronic pain. She said, "It's not about how many times you get rejected or you fall down or you've been beaten up. It's how many times you stand up and are brave and you keep going." That's the kind of attitude and mind-set that is helpful when dealing with something as complicated as trauma.

During her conversation with Oprah, Lady Gaga shared her personal story of being repeatedly raped at age nineteen and how she coped by dissociating from her body. At the time, it served her well. But eventually it caught up with her. It wasn't until she went through trauma treatment that she learned effective ways to cope with the trauma. *The Trauma Map* empowers trauma survivors like Lady Gaga to lead their own healing. It gives step-by-step guidance in a simple and effective way. While I'm not suggesting that this book is a substitute for professional help, it provides an introduction to the first five steps and a bonus sixth step to help you process and heal from your trauma.

People do not deserve to suffer from trauma. They do deserve every opportunity and every tool available to empower themselves to heal and to reconnect with themselves. *The Trauma Map* can be a lifeline for those suffering who are ready to begin a journey of self-discovery, self-healing, and self-love. Oprah Winfrey might have said it best when she said, "Turn your wounds into wisdom."

# Step 1

# Understand Trauma

"Trauma does not just happen to a few unlucky people; it is the bedrock of our psychology. Death and illness touch us all, but even the everyday sufferings of loneliness and fear are traumatic," shared renowned psychiatrist Mark Epstein, author of *The Trauma of Everyday Life.*

I agree with Dr. Epstein—we all experience trauma in one way or another. There is no escaping it. Before we can heal from trauma, we need a better understanding of what trauma is and how much we've endured. By gaining this understanding, we learn how to be more compassionate with ourselves and others.

CHAPTER 1

# Recovery Is Possible

Recovery from trauma is the ultimate goal in trauma treatment. But what that recovery looks like is different for everyone. Ideally, you'll be able to live in the present without being overwhelmed by thoughts and feelings from the past. Before I began treating any patients for trauma, my studies taught me the importance of healing my own trauma before tackling anyone else's. I couldn't be in the present to help others if I wasn't in a good place with my past. This journey of self-discovery allowed me to figure out what methods for trauma treatment might be beneficial to others, and I knew I could stand behind what I recommended for my patients if I held myself to the same standard. I emigrated from Turkey to the United States to attend college at age twenty with a dream to study psychology. I finished my bachelor's degree and then moved forward with my master's degree. I found a master's program in spiritual psychology that focused on self-healing and how you can't help others if you don't heal yourself first.

In the late 1800s, Dr. Pierre Janet created a three-phase framework of trauma recovery that is still extremely relevant today. This book focuses on Phase 1: Stabilization. Stabilization is about feeling safe again. Because of your trauma, you might feel unsafe in the world, in your body, and in relationships with other people. As you work on stabilization, think about it as calming your body. If you are interested in calming yourself in a safe way, this book is for you. I briefly describe each of the three phases below.

> **Phase 1: Stabilization**—Regaining a sense of safety, since people affected by trauma tend to feel unsafe in the world, in their bodies, and in relationships with other people. This phase involves finding ways to calm your nervous system, which most likely has been compromised since the first time you experienced trauma.

> **Phase 2: Trauma Memory Processing**—Processing the trauma to make some meaning out of it. Processing doesn't mean reliving the trauma or even sharing the story without emotion. Instead, it's about looking at what losses happened as a result of the trauma and being able to grieve and express the emotions surrounding what happened.

> **Phase 3: Integration**—Creating a new sense of self and being able to function once the effects of trauma don't hurt you anymore.

Stabilization in Phase 1 often gets ignored in traditional trauma treatment. That was the case with my client Gail. Let me share her story with you.

Despite the will to overcome her depression, Gail couldn't. She didn't know why she was sad and frustrated. Since she had experienced a troubled childhood, she thought her depression could be related to that, but she was not sure. As her depression increased, so did her frustration. My job as her therapist was to educate her about why this was happening.

Gail was afraid to meet me the first time. When I saw her in my waiting room, she looked nervous, and I was struck by her sad eyes. Her coloring looked so pale, and I knew this was not only her fair skin but also a sign of her depression. I welcomed her and we went to my office. Gail had set up quite a few appointments and then canceled at the last minute. I wondered why today she didn't cancel and chose to meet with me. Her beautiful long brown hair was covering most of her eyes. It was obvious that she didn't want to make eye contact with me.

She felt more comfortable writing her thoughts down than speaking them, so she handed me a handwritten note where she shared that she had been struggling with nightmares, flashbacks, fear of sexual intimacy, and irritability. She had been sober from painkillers for about a year. She was afraid to relapse because she had failed attempts at sobriety in the past. After her last detox, Gail was told by her psychiatrist that she wouldn't stay sober, despite her strong will, because her trauma was getting in her way. The psychiatrist recommended that she be specifically treated for her trauma, not for a symptom of it—her addiction. That was why she was meeting with me.

She was not sure why trauma treatment was so important. She believed the trauma had happened too long ago to still matter, let alone be such a big deal. I started our session by explaining what trauma is. She then asked me, "Do I have to tell you what happened to me when I was a child?"

Before doing any emotional work, such as talking about memories, you need to have emotional support. I tell my clients to make a list of their resources. Resources are emotional support tools that they know will make them feel better. These resources can be physical, outer resources or mental, internal resources. Outer resources are people, animals, places, objects, or hobbies that make you feel better. Inner resources include mindfulness techniques, spirituality or religion, and recalling positive memories. Make sure you write your list of resources down, so you can easily reference it later. Just like Gail, many clients tell me they are scared to talk about their feelings. They are sometimes told by therapists that they can't be helped with their trauma symptoms because each time they talk about what happened, they get severely overwhelmed and dissociated. By the time they come to me, they feel hopeless. I give them hope by telling them that trauma work doesn't mean you have to talk about what happened. They are quite surprised by my statement.

I responded to Gail's question, "Let's not talk about trauma yet. We will get to it later when the right time comes. Tell me something you like to do instead of being in therapy." I learned that she was an amazing painter. Art was her absolute passion and purpose in life. She even sold some of her paintings at art galleries. However, lately, she hardly left her home and was unable to sleep. She didn't know the reasons behind her debilitating mood, but she had been told that she might have post-traumatic stress disorder (PTSD), a psychiatric disorder that can happen with people who have experienced or witnessed a shocking, scary, or dangerous event.

As a therapist, I educated her about taking her time and not telling me everything at once. Just like Gail, you might think you have to share all the details of your story, but often that can make you feel worse rather than helping you. I let my clients know that sometimes sharing these details can be retraumatizing for them. Some, like Gail, are terrified to share any information. During this first meeting with Gail, I was more focused on building trust and decreasing her anxiety. If you do seek professional help, don't rush to share details of the trauma right away.

Gail seemed to blame herself for her trauma. In fact, she felt so ashamed that she didn't tell anyone about what had happened to her until she was thirty-seven years old and in rehab. Prior to disclosing the truth, she desperately wanted to shut down her feelings and disconnect from her body. With the help of painkillers, she found an effective way to check out and not deal with painful memories and emotions. As I explained how most trauma victims deal with their past, she seemed curious to know more about trauma and its impact.

Gail fit the profile of having complex PTSD. She had severe anxiety on a daily basis. She often had a hard time breathing. Her body shook; her hands were sweaty. She felt restless and often isolated. Besides intrusive thoughts about her past, she had regular nightmares. She struggled with boundaries, couldn't say no, and therefore often chose to be alone. She'd had only one romantic relationship with a man—years before. Since becoming sober, she had been single and was afraid to date. The more Gail and I talked about her daily struggles, the more I realized how she minimized the impact of her trauma. She believed she should be able to move on, since the trauma had happened years before. The reality was that she could not move on because she had never addressed her traumatic history and didn't realize how disconnected she was from herself.

People often don't understand why they can't get past their trauma, especially if they don't understand what trauma is. To fully understand what is happening to you, you need to understand what trauma is. My first step was to educate Gail about trauma.

# CHAPTER 2

## How Trauma Impacts You

Just like Gail, many of my clients are frustrated because they haven't been able to overcome their trauma on their own. After all, they are strong, smart, capable people. I tell them to stop blaming themselves. Trauma is not something they can overcome with their heads.

According to the American Psychological Association, trauma is an emotional response to a terrible event, such as an accident, rape, or natural disaster. Immediately after the event, shock and denial are typical. Longer-term reactions include unpredictable emotions, flashbacks, strained relationships, and even physical symptoms like headaches or nausea. While these feelings are normal, some people have difficulty moving on with their lives. Psychologists can help these individuals find constructive ways of managing their emotions.[1]

---

[1] American Psychological Association, "Trauma," APA, 2020, https://www.apa.org/topics/trauma/, accessed November 24, 2019.

Trauma may leave you feeling powerless, helpless, and paralyzed. It tends to be sudden and overwhelming; it "owns" you. You cannot think clearly during and after a trauma. If you are overwhelmed by the threat and unable to successfully defend yourself, you can become stuck in survival mode. Trauma might show up in your life in many ways. If you are curious about how trauma has impacted your life, go to the appendix and fill out the Life Events Checklist.

Gail mentioned that she'd had a troubled childhood and also experienced nightmares, which indicates that she'd suffered trauma. I started educating her about how much this was still influencing her today. Gail got curious; it seemed like this was the first time she was hearing about what trauma really was.

## What Constitutes Trauma?

There are many types of trauma. The following are some of the most common types:

- **Relational Trauma:** This type of trauma is the least understood yet the most powerful. Relational trauma might stem from the loss of a loved one, having an emotionally absent parent, or being raised by an abusive parent. Living with a narcissistic or aggressive partner or family member can also create trauma.
- **Medical Trauma:** The impact of a life-changing medical diagnosis, such as cancer, Alzheimer's disease, or another long-term illness, can be a trauma. Surgery, spending a lot of time in the hospital, or having many medical procedures can be very traumatic as well.

- **Physical Trauma:** Injuries from car accidents, falls, and other extreme events can result in flashbacks and additional trauma symptoms.
- **Natural Disasters:** Experiencing events that are out of your control, including pandemics, earthquakes, floods, hurricanes, and other extreme weather events, can cause trauma.
- **Acts of Violence:** Being a victim of crime, rape, assault, or robbery, or witnessing such acts, can cause trauma.
- **Military Service:** Experiencing combat or other traumatic incidents while serving in the military can result in trauma.
- **Racial Trauma:** Race-based traumatic stress is the mental and emotional injury caused by encounters with racial bias and ethnic discrimination, racism, and hate crimes.

You might be surprised to learn how many of us are affected by trauma but don't realize it. According to the research of clinical psychiatrist Bessel van der Kolk, 75 percent of Americans suffer from some type of past traumatic experience.[2] Trauma comes in many forms, and so do people's responses to it. What's important to remember is that someone looking like they have it all together on the outside doesn't mean everything's okay on the inside.

## The Many Faces of Trauma

Once you recognize that you *are traumatized*, you can ask for help. This is the first step in healing. Understanding what trauma does to your well-being reduces the shame and self-blame. Often, when

[2] Finding Mastery, "Dr. Bessel van der Kolk, Trauma Expert," Finding Mastery, 2020, https://findingmastery.net/bessel-van-der-kolk, accessed August 3, 2020.

people think about trauma, they consider only "big traumas," such as rape and war. If they did not experience such a "big trauma," they may not believe they too are suffering from trauma. That couldn't be further from the truth.

Trauma and violence are widespread, harmful, and costly public health concerns. Sadly, trauma impacts many more of us than most people realize, and the effects of this trauma are wide-reaching and life-altering. Consider these alarming statistics:

- A 2008 RAND Corporation study found that 18.5 percent of returning veterans reported symptoms consistent with post-traumatic stress disorder or depression.[3]
- According to the U.S. Department of Veterans Affairs, 11 to 20 percent of veterans who fought in Afghanistan or Iraq have suffered from PTSD, while roughly 30 percent of Vietnam War veterans have suffered from PTSD.[4]
- In the United States, 18.9 percent of men and 15.2 percent of women reported a lifetime experience of a natural disaster.[5]

Research shows that experiencing trauma increases the risk of mental illness, physical health problems, violence, and substance

[3] M. A. Burnam, L. S. Meredith, T. Tanielian, and L. Jaycox, "Improving Mental Health Care for Returning Veterans," Rand Corporation, 2009, https://www.rand.org/pubs/research_briefs/RB9451.html, accessed August 20, 2020.

[4] National Center for PTSD, "How Common Is PTSD in Veterans?" U.S. Department of Veterans Affairs, September 24, 2018, https://www.ptsd.va.gov/understand/common/common_veterans.asp, accessed August 14, 2020.

[5] R. C. Kessler, A. Sonnega, E. Bromet, M. Hughes, and C. B. Nelson., "Posttraumatic Stress Disorder in the National Comorbidity Survey," *Arch Gen Psychiatry* 52, no. 12 (December 1995): 1048–60, https://pubmed.ncbi.nlm.nih.gov/7492257/, accessed August 22, 2020.

abuse. These behavioral health issues can make almost every aspect of life more difficult—one's career, ability to cope with challenges, relationships with others, and, most importantly, relationship with oneself. With the spotlight of the #MeToo movement on sexual trauma, in particular, we as a society are beginning to understand the widespread incidence and long-term effects of trauma on people's lives. The good news is that it is possible to heal from trauma. You can find your way back to the person you know you are deep down inside.

Many people think trauma requires a physical component such as a war, accident, or natural disaster. That's simply not the case. Relational trauma is one of the most common underestimated traumas. When the bonding and healthy attachment between a parent and child get disrupted, that's relational trauma. A child who has been neglected can in fact suffer from more emotional symptoms than a rape victim. Relational trauma that happens in childhood can be just as traumatic.

Van der Kolk explains, "The impact of neglect or abandonment is greater than sexual abuse. Children who do not have healthy attachments have been shown to be more vulnerable to stress." One of my clients grew up with an emotionally absent mom. There was no physical abuse in her childhood, but she suffered with fears of abandonment all her life. Children need more than food to survive—they need emotional attunement.

Your first relationship with your caregivers impacts not only your relationship with others but your relationships with yourself as well. Secure attachment to an adult teaches your nervous system how to regulate. You learn that you are never alone and can weather any storm of emotions. First relationships teach you how to create a safe zone with someone or with yourself. That is the first view of your world.

## Childhood Trauma

Oprah Winfrey addressed the long-term effects of childhood trauma on the March 11, 2018, episode of *60 Minutes*, where she talked about her own sexual trauma. Dr. Nadine Burke Harris's TED Talk "How Childhood Trauma Affects Health across a Lifetime" has gone viral. Her talk relates to research on adverse childhood experiences and how they can impact future violence, victimization, and perpetration, and as well as lifelong health and opportunity.

According to the CDC–Kaiser Permanente Adverse Childhood Experiences (ACE) Study, conducted from 1995 to 1997,[6] traumatic events that happen during childhood, from age zero to seventeen, can have a lasting impact. Such events include experiencing violence, abuse, or neglect; witnessing violence in the home; or having a family member attempt or die from suicide. A child's environment may undermine their sense of safety and bonding. Growing up in a dysfunctional household with substance abuse, mental health problems, or instability can have a serious impact on someone's future as an adult. This can include:

- Risky behavior
- Chronic health problems
- Low life potential
- Premature death

---

[6] Center for Disease Control and Prevention, "Injury Prevention and Control: Division of Violence Prevention," CDC, http:/www.cdc.gov/violenceprevention/acestudy/index.html, accessed September 1, 2020 .

Your risk factor depends on how many ACEs you have. To determine what your risk factors are, you can calculate your ACE score by taking a short quiz found in the appendix. But note, some of these questions can be triggering.

A surprising two-thirds of the seventeen thousand people in the ACE Study had an ACE score of at least 1; 87 percent of those had a score higher than 1.

The study showed that:

- Childhood trauma is very common, even among employed, white middle-class, college-educated people with great health insurance.
- There is a direct link between childhood trauma and adult onset of chronic disease, as well as a link with depression, suicide, being violent, and being a victim of violence.
- More types of trauma increase the risk of health, social, and emotional problems.
- People usually experience more than one type of trauma—rarely is it only sexual abuse or only verbal abuse.

We are just now learning the impact of childhood trauma and how it plays out in our daily lives..

## Collective Trauma

Something we can all relate to is collective trauma. In March 2020, much of the world shut down due to the COVID-19 pandemic. When stay-at-home orders were first issued, reactions varied. Most people worried to some degree about their health and their financial future. However, there were also extreme reactions. There were people in denial, those minimizing what was happening, and those using humor to avoid it. At the other end of the spectrum were those who were not only distressed by the crisis but also plagued with memories of past traumas. This group in particular struggled with debilitating anxiety and depression.

During the pandemic, depression and anxiety increased for survivors of past trauma, since any current stressor can trigger memories and feelings of past trauma. For example, someone who comes from a broken home might struggle with community stay-at-home orders. Being forced to stay at home as an adult might trigger childhood memories of being unable to escape dysfunction or emotional or physical abuse. People who were frequently sick in childhood and felt powerless might have similar feelings of powerlessness during illness in the pandemic. Worries about finances might stir memories of witnessing domestic violence after a parent lost a job.

Bouts of stress, depression, and anxiousness that many normally feel in response to a crisis become greater for someone already struggling with trauma. Here are some reasons why:

1. **Crises are sudden and unpredictable.** Nobody knows what to expect. That can be disconcerting for anyone, but for someone with a history of trauma, a current crisis can create more stress. Trauma itself is usually sudden and unpredictable. This is true, for example, for anyone who experienced inconsistent parenting and crises because of living with an alcoholic or mentally unstable parent. A current crisis can cause that person to feel like they are back in childhood with a violent, abusive, or neglectful parent.
2. **Confusion.** Lack of information, misinformation, or conflicting information can trigger stress in anyone. When leadership gives mixed messages, everyone becomes more confused.

3. **Feeling out of control.** Anyone who experienced trauma didn't have control over the situation. COVID-19 brought that same feeling of being out of control: we relied on doctors and scientists to control the pandemic but could do nothing but take safety precautions, such as washing our hands, wearing masks, and social distancing.
4. **Feeling like it's never going to end.** When there is not a predictable endpoint to something, it can feel like it's going to last forever. And that can stir feelings of hopelessness.
5. **Grief.** Anyone can feel grief, even if they have never experienced trauma. To one degree or another, everyone is grieving for what life once was: the "old normal." With social distancing and shelter-in-place orders, every community has lost a sense of normalcy. For children, this can be especially challenging, as they don't understand why they no longer can be with their friends or play at the playground.
6. **Isolation.** As humans, we aren't meant to be alone. We need connection with others. Social distancing has caused many people to isolate and, as a result, feel disconnected from others, and perhaps even from themselves.
7. **Addiction.** Many people who already struggle with addiction may find it easier to fall back into or increase addictive behavior. Being isolated from others can cause people to lose their sense of purpose, so they look for comfort in alcohol or other drugs.

## How Do I Know If I'm Suffering from Trauma?

If you are experiencing any of the feelings below, you might be suffering from trauma.

- Shock, including numbed emotions, questioning of perceptions, and memory disturbances
- Denial, which helps reduce terror, feelings of helplessness, and a fear of dying or being abandoned to manageable levels
- Hyperarousal, increased heart rate, or racing thoughts
- Confusion and disorientation
- Numbness
- Panic
- Dissociation or feelings of unreality
- Unwanted thoughts or traumatic memories intruding on everyday living and dreams, leaving you feeling out of control
- Trouble sleeping
- Feeling helpless
- Hypervigilance (being on guard all the time)
- Nightmares or night terrors
- Mood swings
- A reduced ability to deal with stress
- Fear of going crazy
- Anxiety
- Depression
- Mental blankness or feeling spacey
- Difficulty concentrating
- Forgetfulness
- Inability to love or nurture others
- Inability to make commitments
- Immune system and endocrine problems

Trauma is like a barrier between you and your emotions. No two people experience or manifest trauma in exactly the same way. When you are traumatized, you need support, not judgment. PTSD can be the result of trauma, as it was for my client Gail. She shared, without going into specific details, that she had suffered sexual abuse as a child. She realized that she was dismissing this important event in her life. However, when she understood the severity of what trauma was and understood her condition better, she took a deep sigh at the end of the session.

## How Do I Know If I Have PTSD?

PTSD, a serious and potentially debilitating condition, can occur in those who have experienced or witnessed a natural disaster, serious accident, terrorist incident, sudden death of a loved one, war, violent personal assault such as rape, or another traumatic event.

During this type of event, you think your life or another's life is in danger. Not every trauma turns into PTSD, however. Most people who experience traumatic events recover from them. But people with PTSD continue to be severely depressed and anxious for months or years following the event. PTSD can happen to anyone. It is not a sign of weakness. About seven or eight people out of every one hundred will have PTSD at some point in their lives. About eight million adults have PTSD during a given year. This is only a small portion of those who have gone through trauma.[7]

The main difference between PTSD and the experience of trauma is that a traumatic event is time-based, while PTSD is a longer-term condition where someone continues to have flashbacks and reexperiences the traumatic event over and over again. Besides meeting these criteria for PTSD, a high level of ongoing distress and life impairment must be present.

---

[7] National Center for PTSD, "How Common Is PTSD in Adults?" U.S. Department of Veterans Affairs, https://www.ptsd.va.gov/understand/common/common_adults.asp, accessed August 14, 2020.

The words we use to describe PTSD have changed over the years. Originally, the language was intended to describe soldiers in combat. In 1761 Austrian physician Josef Leopold wrote about "nostalgia" among soldiers. Among those who were exposed to military trauma, some reported missing home, feeling sad, sleep problems, and anxiety. Later, a "soldier's heart" or "irritable heart" was characterized by a rapid pulse, anxiety, and trouble breathing. During World War I, the condition was referred to as shell shock, as it was viewed as a reaction to the explosion of artillery shells. In World War II, the shell shock diagnosis was replaced by the term *combat stress reaction*, also known as battle fatigue. It wasn't until 1980 that the American Psychiatric Association added PTSD to it diagnostic manual, which helps clinicians diagnose mental disorders. This came about from research involving returning Vietnam War veterans, Holocaust survivors, sexual trauma victims, and others.[8]

According to the National Alliance on Mental Illness (NAMI), the more someone tries not to think about a traumatic event, resists revisiting a traumatic place, and avoids contact with any potential triggers of the traumatic event, the more likely they are to develop PTSD.

If you are wondering whether PTSD might be an issue for you, you can take a short quiz called the Abbreviated PCL-C in the appendix.

---

[8] National Center for PTSD, "History of PTSD in Veterans: Civil War to DSM-5," U.S. Department of Veterans Affairs, October 17, 2019, https://www.ptsd.va.gov/understand/what/history_ptsd.asp, accessed August 14, 2020.

## PTSD and the Military

People in the military who find themselves haunted by memories might feel a tremendous amount of shame, since they've been trained to be strong. They might become frustrated that they have the physical strength to endure boot camp but can't beat trauma. The result is sometimes suicide. In September 2019, the Department of Veterans Affairs reported an average of seventeen veteran suicides each day and noted rising suicide rates between 2016 and 2017.[9]

The documentary *The Invisible War* features male and female veterans who were sexually abused by their fellow soldiers. After meeting with the directors, I created the Invisible War Recovery Program for veterans suffering from military sexual trauma (MST). Two groups of six female veterans who were sexual abuse survivors enrolled in the program. In the first group, five of the six women had also been abused as children.

The one woman who had supportive parents and a healthier childhood and wasn't abused as a child was able to overcome the trauma more easily than the other five women. However, the other women needed to go back to their childhood traumas to heal from the traumas they experienced in the military.

## Why You Often Can't Shake Trauma

Trauma is complicated, and people have a tendency to beat themselves up if they can't just "get over" it. They either blame themselves for not being able to fight off their perpetrator or believe they

---

[9] U.S. Department of Veterans Affairs, "Mental Health," U.S. Department of Veterans Affairs, June 22, 2020, https://www.mentalhealth.va.gov/mentalhealth/suicide_prevention/data.asp, accessed August 14, 2020.

should have already moved on, especially if the trauma happened a long time ago. They often feel that time should heal everything. I'm here to tell you that this is not how it works with trauma. Time does *not* heal everything. When trauma happens, it gets stuck in our brain. That particular trauma is like a time capsule in your mind. It has nothing to do with you not being strong or intelligent enough. In other words, when trauma happens, the cognitive brain doesn't function. You feel everything on an emotional and physical level. You're heightened to survival mode. You get stuck because you haven't digested what happened.

If you are frozen in a certain time frame, years later, if there is a reminder of a traumatic event, all of a sudden you go back to that moment. For example, one of my clients, Keisha, was abused when she was a child by her alcoholic father, who would often drink beer while driving. Years later Keisha was driving in a car and her friend in the passenger seat opened a can of soda. The noise sounded exactly like her father opening a can of beer in the car—a situation that would eventually turn into some sort of abusive act. Keisha instantly went into a severe flashback and panic attack because her brain did not know the difference between past and present. This is what it is like to be frozen in time. People who blame themselves for being unable to move on from a traumatic event might be relieved to learn this. Now they understand why they can't sleep or are having anxiety. It's the trauma that keeps pulling them back in time.

At the Sandy Hook Elementary School in Newtown, Connecticut, on December 14, 2012, twenty-year-old Adam Lanza shot and killed twenty-six people: twenty children and six adult staff members. As first responders arrived at the school, Lanza killed himself.

One of my clients, Patricia, was a highly functioning, successful teacher at Sandy Hook with a happy marriage and a great life. After the school shooting, her life changed drastically, although she wasn't physically wounded by a bullet.

After December 14, 2012, she became homebound. She couldn't go back to work as a teacher and could no longer travel—something she and her husband had thoroughly enjoyed. Panic attacks and nightmares filled her days and nights. She was no longer herself and couldn't enjoy things she had appreciated in the past. She couldn't understand why some of her fellow teachers were doing fine while she couldn't get past the event. The key difference? Patricia's friends had never endured childhood trauma. As a child, Patricia was physically abused by her father. She had never fully worked through these feelings.

Patricia didn't know that she was traumatized not only by the school shooting; she had childhood trauma as well. We could now start our therapy work—tying her childhood trauma to what happened at the school shooting. That's when it became apparent that her childhood trauma was deeply connected to the event. By understanding this, she was able to start healing. We helped her process the childhood memories, which allowed her to get back to living life. When you have a chronic childhood trauma and then trauma occurs in your adult life, you will be impacted in a much deeper way than someone who never experienced childhood trauma. You can't disregard your whole life story. You have to validate and understand your whole life. It all has meaning.

## The Ramifications of Childhood Sexual Abuse

About 90 percent of my clients experienced childhood sexual abuse. Often, that abuse was from parents, grandparents, uncles, close family friends, or neighbors. Perpetrators come in many shapes and sizes and from all walks of life. One of my clients, Yolanda, was abused from age nine to about thirteen. Eventually Yolanda and her family moved to another country, where she was now safe, which helped her to share what had happened with her parents. Her parents were extremely religious and instead of comforting her for what she had endured, they told her she couldn't live with hatred in her heart and needed to forgive the perpetrators.

Yolanda experienced what's called a spiritual bypass—she was not allowed to grieve. She went from disclosing the abuse to immediately forgiving the perpetrators in the name of God. Despite forgiving, she was never able to forget what had happened. She grew up, eventually married, and had children. Then she started having flashbacks and didn't know what to do. That's when she realized she hadn't actually forgiven her perpetrators. To cope with these feelings, she started smoking marijuana. It became a regular coping mechanism.

When she became a client at Reconnect, we helped Yolanda realize that the experiences she'd had were quite traumatic and that was why she couldn't simply move on and quiet her mind. For the first time she felt understood and validated. She had felt so judged before. Everything started making sense. Her nightmares and depression finally made sense to her. She now understood that a spiritual bypass of trauma doesn't work. She couldn't forgive without processing her feelings. Now she was ready and able to deal with the initial trauma in order to reconnect with herself and others.

Now that you understand a little more about trauma, we can go on to the next step. I'll start by teaching you how to reconnect with your brain. Think of your brain as your control center.

## Ten Points to Remember

1. Understand what trauma means.
2. Understand how trauma impacted you.
3. Accept that trauma occurred.
4. Remember that trauma was not your fault.
5. Know that your emotions about the trauma are stuck in your emotional brain.
6. Remember that your rational brain shuts down when there is a threat.
7. Accept your limitations as a traumatized person.
8. Remember that trauma = disconnect; healing = reconnect
9. Be gentle with yourself.
10. Don't hesitate to ask for extra support if you need professional help.

"The secret of health for both mind and body is not to mourn for the past, nor to worry about the future, but to live the present moment wisely and earnestly."

—Siddhartha Gautama

# Step 2

# Reconnect to Your Mind

During and after a traumatic event, your brain shuts down and it becomes very difficult to think straight and make decisions. Trauma clouds the way you think. Once we understand more about what happens in the brain, we can begin to connect the dots on what happens when we are traumatized and how and why we respond the way we do.

CHAPTER 3

# Trauma and the Brain

To understand what happens to you after trauma, it is helpful to understand how your brain functions.

In 1967 neuroscientist Paul D. MacLean formulated a model called the triune brain; he described the brain as having three distinct parts. Although this model is a highly simplified explanation of brain activity, it provides an easy-to-understand hierarchy of brain functions.

1. **Reptilian brain.** This part of the brain is responsible for the most basic survival functions, such as heart rate, breathing, body temperature, and body sensations. When we are in danger and must respond quickly, the reptilian brain is aroused, preparing us for action by initiating the release of chemicals throughout the body. The functions of this part of the brain take precedence over other brain activity. For example, if you try to hold your breath, the reptilian brain will take over and make you breathe again.

2. **Emotional brain (limbic system).** The limbic system is where emotions and somatic memories are stored. It is also the reactive part of the brain; it initiates the "fight or flight" response to danger to keep us safe. When we watch a shocking news story or receive an upsetting message, the limbic system is stimulated and chemicals are released, creating our emotions.
3. **Rational brain (frontal cortex).** The frontal cortex is responsible for all executive and cognitive functioning activities, such as language, abstract thought, imagination, and creativity. When we make decisions, solve problems, or reason, we use the frontal cortex. When we are faced with trauma, the rational brain can be "hijacked" by the emotional brain. In other words, the rational brain can "go offline" as blood flow is directed to the deeper limbic system, the first responder to keep us safe.

Dr. Daniel Siegel, a world-famous neuroscientist and professor, developed the hand model of the brain to explain how emotions and trauma overwhelm the brain.

Start by holding your hand up, folding your thumb in, and closing your fingers down in a fist. When you become angry or scared, it's like opening the fist. Think of it as "flipping your lid." You become overwhelmed and are unable to think clearly. The emotional part of the brain doesn't understand complex thoughts; it is intrinsic and animalistic.

The exercises in this book, such as mindfulness and grounding techniques, will allow you to develop more frontal cortex activity in the thinking brain, which will eventually help calm your nervous system.

Hoping to be inspirational, someone once posted on Facebook, "Although we can't always choose what happens to us, we can always choose how to respond." But for some of my clients, the post

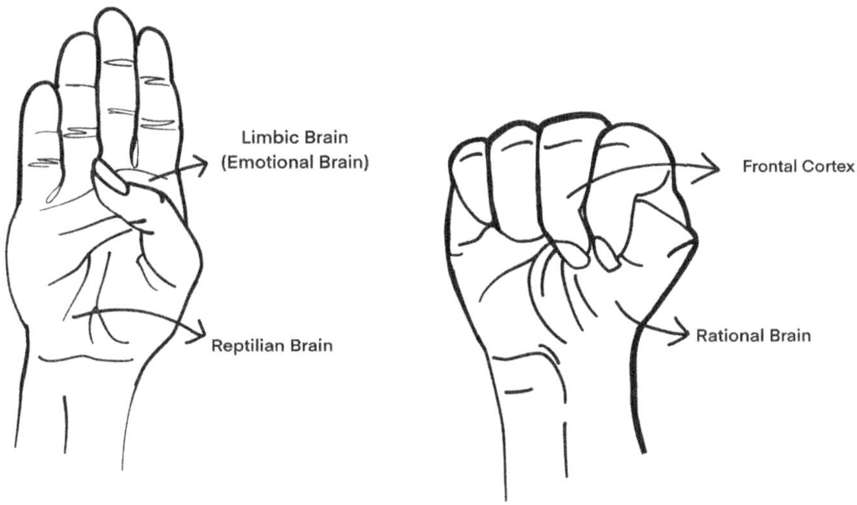


was the opposite of inspirational. While those can be empowering words, they triggered a lot of people in a negative way. One person commented, "This statement is false. Fight, flight, or freeze behaviors are unconsciously reflexive. We need to stop perpetuating the myth that we are always in conscious control of our actions. It hurts and shames children and adults." The person who commented was right. In the moment of a traumatic event, we are not in control of our reaction. That's why, in the beginning phase of trauma treatment, through a process called psychoeducation, I educate my clients about what often happens when we are traumatized.

I explained to my client Theresa, "During a traumatic event, the thinking brain shuts down and makes it impossible for us to think straight. Our first goal is to explore how you are disconnected from your mind and thoughts, and how to reconnect to your mind again." I was hoping to gain her confidence and trust, and to help minimize her shame. I also knew that Theresa didn't want to feel her feelings. That's why she had been drinking heavily for many years. I knew that if we started talking about her thoughts rather than feelings, she could tolerate the sessions better.

I shared, "When you are traumatized, your rational brain gets deactivated and your reptilian or emotional brain becomes active. This helps you to fight, flee, or freeze. You aren't thinking. It's an instinct. That's why you can't think clearly when you are triggered or traumatized. You become speechless. Trauma gets imprinted on the emotional brain. The emotional brain hijacks your rational self. Your heart starts pounding, you start breathing faster, and your voice changes."

After sharing this with Theresa, I asked, "How are you feeling now? Do you have any questions?" She responded, "I am actually feeling better. I am not sure why, but what you shared so far helps me feel better and less crazy." I said, "I understand. That's why I took the time to tell you about what trauma is and what it does to you. Your symptoms are very common based on your history. Many trauma survivors tend to minimize their symptoms or feel too ashamed to get help. Most of the time that's because of the stigma associated with mental illness."

Now that I had her attention, I continued: "Do you know that a lot of trauma victims blame themselves for not fighting back during the trauma? Did that ever happen to you?" Theresa gave me a puzzled look and said, "What do you mean?" I said, "Did you ever blame yourself for the childhood abuse or feel it was your fault that your father left?" She lowered her face.

My client Robin has a black belt in karate. She was sexually assaulted and froze during the attack, as many victims do. Robin was very angry at herself afterward for not fighting off the perpetrator. She couldn't understand why she hadn't. Others were also surprised because of her vigorous self-defense training. She felt great shame about not fighting back. She didn't know that at the moment of a perceived threat, you will automatically do one of three things: fight, flee, or freeze.

Adrenaline pumps through your veins. After the threat goes away, it can take up to an hour for your heart rate, blood pressure, and breathing to return to normal.

In prehistoric times, a caveman had to make quick decisions when outrunning a predator such as a lion. With the fight, flight, or freeze response, there's no time to think about what to do. Your body just responds. Your cognitive brain shuts down, which limits your capacity to think. Your body simply naturally responds in the way it knows best and is most comfortable with—it fights back, takes flight, or freezes.

Later, when she could think rationally, Robin thought about all the strategies she could have used against her attacker. Keep in mind that during the trauma, her rational brain was flooded with stress chemicals, making the situation feel completely out of her control. Only by learning how the brain works was she able to forgive herself for freezing during the attack.

Brain scans of trauma survivors are different than brain scans of those who have never experienced trauma. In studies of brain imaging, PTSD has been associated with impaired function in multiple regions of the brain.[10] Each part of the brain plays a role in memory storage and emotional processing, and the brains of people with PTSD are adversely affected long term by the increased stress hormones released.[11]

---

[10] J. Douglas Bremner, "Neuroimaging in Posttraumatic Stress Disorder and Other Stress-Related Disorders," *Neuroimaging Clinics of North America* 17, no. 4 (November 2007): 523–38, https://www.ncbi.nlm.nih.gov/pmc/articles/PMC2729089/#R105, accessed August 14, 2020.

[11] J. Douglas Bremner, "Traumatic Stress: Effects on the Brain," *Dialogues in Clinical Neuroscience* 8, no. 4 (December 2006): 445–61, https://www.ncbi.nlm.nih.gov/pmc/articles/PMC3181836/, accessed August 14, 2020.

As I explained this to Theresa, she lifted her head and made eye contact with me. I was choosing every word carefully to make sure she understood what was happening in her brain. Listening to Theresa and educating her about trauma laid the foundation for our therapeutic relationship. During the following sessions, my goal was to empower her. I knew that one way to do that was to show her what she could do differently to overcome some of the traumatic symptoms she was dealing with. I asked, "Besides your father, mother, and uncle, who else mistreated you and hurt you this way? Who else abandoned you?" She responded, "I think I was bullied at school too."

I asked, "Who else treated you badly?"

"That's it, I think," she said with a puzzled look on her face. I assured her that the trauma she had experienced was severe, and then I asked my favorite question: "How is your relationship with yourself? How have you been treating yourself?"

There was a long pause. Then there was a shift in the room, a sense of new insight coming into her thoughts, as was evident in her eyes. She responded, "Not very good, I'm afraid. I have not been treating myself well at all." After a few seconds of silence, she said, "Oh, now I understand why you were asking me who else treated me badly. The answer is *me*! I have not been nice to myself at all. In fact, I have been my own worst enemy at times."

For most of my clients, this is an aha moment, just like it was for Theresa.

"To heal the past, you first have to look at how your relationship with yourself is *now*," I continued. Past trauma leaves an imprint on how you treat yourself. If you were abused, you may abuse yourself. If you were abandoned, you may abandon yourself. Trauma creates disconnect within. The goal is to improve your relationship with yourself.

*Dis*connecting from yourself means losing who you are, losing your sense of purpose, and living in pain. If you were abused as a child, chances are good you grew up hearing very negative things about who you are. Eventually you believed them, as if they were your own thoughts. Trauma may make you give up on yourself. Take a good look at how you are treating yourself. If you treated other people the way you treat yourself, would they be okay with that? Why or why not?

While your trauma happened in the past, the impact of it is felt now. Before you can heal the past, you must make sure you are connected to the present—the here and now. You can't change the past. But there's something you can do to help you in the here and now to feel better.

Before talking about making changes, let's look at why it is sometimes so difficult to make changes. Often, it's because you don't even realize the full extent of your trauma. Or maybe you compensate in other ways, like negative self-talk and seeking perfection. You can't connect the dots when you are disconnected.

CHAPTER 4

# What Happens When You Are Disconnected?

The majority of my clients who've experienced trauma don't recall details of the trauma or even the actual event. One client, Desiree, was sexually abused by a distant family member at a very young age. She didn't remember until she was thirty years old.

She was watching TV and saw someone being abused. Suddenly, she started having flashbacks and nightmares about what had happened to her as a child. She went into a state of shock: one day she remembered nothing, and on the next she saw herself being abused as a child. When something like this happens, people might begin doubting themselves because the denial is so strong.

In a 2014 article in *Time* magazine, Dr. James Hopper of Harvard Medical School and researcher Dr. David Lisak looked at why rape and trauma survivors have incomplete memories. They explained that the part of the brain that processes rational thought can actually shut down in times of extremely high stress or fear. Essentially, when we need the rational brain the most, it can be incapacitated by a surge of stress chemicals, such as cortisol.[12] So instead of taking a rational course of action, in the face of an emergency, we effectively freeze. And because the brain is not able to make logical sense of what is happening, later we may not be able to remember details about the event. Hopper and Lisak explained that it is normal for the brain to react this way.[13] And when people can't remember what has happened to them, they often doubt themselves.

## How Can You Tell If You Are Disconnected from Your Mind?

The following are signs that you might be disconnected from your mind:

- Perfectionism
- Negative self-talk
- Loss of purpose
- Difficulty concentrating
- Memory loss
- Difficulty making decisions
- Avoidance symptoms

---

[12] Vanessa A. van Ast, Sandra Cornelisse, Martijn Meeter, and Merel Kindt, "Time-Dependent Effects of Cortisol on the Contextualization of Emotion Memories," *Biological Psychiatry* 74, no. 11 (December 1, 2013): 809–16, https://www.sciencedirect.com/science/article/abs/pii/S0006322313006410, accessed August 14, 2020.

[13] James Hopper and David Lisak, "Why Rape and Trauma Survivors Have Fragmented and Incomplete Memories," *Time*, December 9, 2014, https://time.com/3625414/rape-trauma-brain-/, accessed August 14, 2020.

## Perfectionism

A lot of people suffer from the desire to be perfect and don't realize how hurtful this can be to their self-esteem. You may feel like no matter what you do, you are never good enough. You may spend all your energy and time trying to make others happy.

My client Jorge was a highly successful businessman. At age ten he was forced to take on the role of an adult as his family was breaking apart. This is traumatic for a child. Instead of just being a kid, Jorge felt that his self-worth and how much his family loved him depended on his ability to achieve. This type of mentality continued into adulthood. He was a high achiever and hard worker. He achieved a lot. He got married to the woman of his dreams and adored the children they produced. But something was missing. Because of his desire for achievement, he began neglecting his wife, children, and health. He soon discovered that being successful in business was costing him his life. Jorge became my client when he realized he wasn't ready to give up his life without a fight.

## Negative Self-Talk

This is a very common symptom. You may tell yourself that you are stupid, worthless, fat, or ugly. Traumatized people struggle with self-compassion because of deep shame and self-hatred.

My client Julia was a single parent of two boys. As a child, she was physically and sexually abused. As a result, she had symptoms of PTSD. Like Jorge, she was successful at work, but she couldn't stop thinking about what had happened to her as a child. While logically she knew that the past was in the past and she was safe now, she had recurring nightmares that made her angry. She kept asking, "Why can't I get past this?" I asked about her kids, who both have autism. "Do you get angry with your kids when they don't behave in a certain way?" She replied, "No." "Why don't you judge and get upset with them?" I asked. "Because the brains of people with autism process information differently than those of neurotypical people. They have different brain chemistry. I understand that, so I don't get upset. They can't help it," she replied.

I asked, "Have you ever thought that your brain's chemistry has been altered because you were a victim of trauma?" She burst into tears, realizing that her problems had nothing to do with her not being strong enough or smart enough. Her brain chemistry had changed and it wasn't her fault. That realization made all the difference to her. Now she was able understand why she was struggling so much.

### Loss of Purpose

After trauma you may no longer enjoy things you once liked and therefore feel confused about the direction of your life. When you are hurt, your attention may be focused on the past, making it difficult to figure out a sense of purpose in your life. Trauma can also impact your creativity.

### Difficulty Concentrating

When traumatic memories are overwhelming, you may have a hard time concentrating on other things, as if there is no space left in your brain. Trauma victims often talk about feeling "cloudy" and being flooded with intrusive thoughts or memories.

### Memory Loss

You might have difficulty remembering key parts of your trauma experience—or you may have forgotten the whole incident. You may also struggle with memory loss and have difficulty doing day-to-day chores.

### Difficulty Making Decisions

Trauma impacts intuition and the thinking capacity of the brain. You may have a hard time making decisions because you don't know what feels right or wrong anymore.

### Avoidance Symptoms

You may want to avoid anything that reminds you (an event, conversation, or thought) of the past traumatic event. Often, avoidance causes people to become withdrawn.

The purpose of the following exercise is to help you see how these trauma symptoms are impacting your life.

## Exercise 4.1: Increase Self-Awareness

Review the following list of symptoms, choose the two symptoms you can most relate to, and write down where and when they showed up in your life.

- Perfectionism
- Negative self-talk
- Loss of purpose
- Difficulty concentrating
- Memory loss
- Difficulty making decisions
- Avoidance symptoms

CHAPTER 5

# Make Peace with Yourself

Now that you understand the different ways you can disconnect from your mind, it's time to make peace with yourself by reconnecting to your mind. There are five ways to accomplish this:

1. Challenge the way you talk to yourself
2. Work on self-forgiveness
3. Write internal dialogues
4. Control your thoughts
5. Stay in the present moment

## Challenge the Way You Talk to Yourself

To reconnect to your mind, it is important to stop the negative self-talk. My client Robert was admired by his many friends. It was obvious that he was very loved, but he strongly believed he was unlovable.

I asked him to write down a list of all negative things he said to himself regularly. The next day he brought me his list:

- You are stupid
- This definitely looks ugly on you
- Nobody cares about you
- You acted in a very stupid way, as usual
- You are worthless and everyone can see that

I asked him, "Do you ever say any of these things to your friends? Do you tell them repeatedly that they are ugly, stupid, and worthless?"

"No, of course not!" he said.

"Well, why not?"

Robert exclaimed, "Well, I don't think they would want to be my friends, would they?"

I wanted to take this issue one step further and asked, "Would you let anyone else talk to you in the way you have been talking to yourself?"

"No, I wouldn't for sure," he said, not to my surprise.

"How about if I, as your therapist, said these things to you?"

He seemed even more surprised. "I would not come to you for help," he added without hesitation.

"Now you may reconsider the way you are talking to yourself," I said.

To challenge negative beliefs, you have to be willing to let them go. You have to believe they are your enemies and that you have no other choice but to disregard them. When I first started challenging my negative thoughts, I said to myself, "It doesn't matter whether

I think I am right about the negative thoughts or not, I know that it is not good for me to say these things. I am committed to doing healthy things. So I refuse to repeat these words, and I refuse to believe them."

Then I would hear my judgmental voice inside saying, "But you are not good enough—it is proven—as you get easily upset, you care too much about what others think of you, and you seem strong but are weak."

I would argue back, "That's bullshit. I am not perfect, for sure, but I am okay. I accept myself for who I am, and that is enough."

As I began my self-discovery journey, I became passionate about working on myself. I learned various tools and techniques, and I journaled my thoughts and feelings. As I unpacked what I had been harboring inside for so long, I realized I had spent years fighting against my feelings. By being overly worried about what others thought about me and whether they loved me or not, I constantly abandoned myself. I spent a lot of time thinking about things that were out of my control, and I was highly critical of myself.

While I hated to feel my emotions, I loved to think. As strange as it sounds, I felt safe using my intellect to analyze my experiences and study myself. I approached myself as if I were a case study in one of my psychology books. I analyzed myself, read about psychology, and journaled—challenging my thoughts, exploring my feelings, and processing my memories. I became much more aware of who I had been—and who I was becoming. By the time I finished my doctorate in psychology, I had made good progress. It was very clear to me that my passion was working with childhood trauma, due to my own attachment trauma. It took me quite some time to accept myself fully for who I am.

I learned to accept my past. I made peace with my feelings and quit striving for perfection. I started practicing regular grounding techniques. As a result, I was able to control my negative thoughts by staying in my body and being in the present moment. Using my body was, without a doubt, one of the most important factors in my personal trauma healing.

The following activity will help you see how you treat yourself. It may be the first step in realizing that you need to make a change.

## Exercise 5.1: How Are You Treating Yourself?

List all the ways you have not been treating yourself the way you deserve. Write down some of the most common negative things you say about yourself and how often you say them in a twenty-four-hour period.

Are you surprised at what you say to yourself and how often you say it? Most people are. Being aware is the first step in making a change. Once you have a clear understanding of this issue, the next step is to make a commitment to stop all self-abuse.

---

When I teach clients about the importance of positive self-talk, they often argue with me. For instance, Robert said, "But I can't stop saying bad things to myself because I don't like myself."

I said, "It doesn't matter what you think of yourself. In fact, you don't need to love yourself, but you just can't talk this way. Just know that you are not allowed to talk this way, just like you wouldn't allow anyone else to talk to you in the same insulting way."

You have to be very willing to make this change. When I first started this journey, it didn't matter what I *believed.* I knew that it was unhealthy to judge myself, so I stopped myself each time I had a negative comment about myself. Behind every negative thought about yourself is a lie you were made to believe, whether consciously or subconsciously. A key step is to identify what that lie is. The lie could be that you're worthless, you're a failure, or you're a nobody.

Maybe you were told that you were dumb or that everything is your fault. Whatever the lie is, identify it and write it out. Give it back to whomever it really belongs to.

Often, perpetrators tell lies to their victims. They want victims to believe the abuse is their fault. That way, the perpetrator can feel free of guilt. The only way to combat a lie is with the truth. Now is the time to seek out the truth about you. Ask people who love you why they love you. Explore why you believe lies about yourself. Where is the proof that you are worthless or unlovable? You must be determined to find the truth.

Whatever you were blaming yourself for, would you blame your best friend or a child in the same way? Or would you be more compassionate toward them?

## Work on Self-Forgiveness

When you judge yourself, it creates a lot of inner pain and anger. It is common to talk about forgiving others after they hurt you. In fact, many religions address the importance of forgiveness as a way to achieve peace inside. How about *self*-forgiveness? Can you order a cease-fire inside yourself? Can you accept yourself for who you are, with all your imperfections? Or do you wish you were different? Wishing you were different means wishing the past didn't exist, and that takes you into denial. Accept who you are—accept what happened on a daily basis.

Self-love doesn't mean you change yourself. Self-love means you accept yourself as an imperfect person. Self-love means accepting your faults 100 percent. You can still work on yourself to improve your behaviors, but if you made mistakes in the past, you cannot change that. Don't compare yourself to anyone. You are unique. You are you.

## Exercise 5.2: Practice Self-Forgiveness

Read the poem below, written and graciously shared here by a colleague of mine, and then journal your feelings about it.

**"Self-Forgiveness"**
**by Kurt Christiansen, PsyD**

I forgive myself.
I forgive myself for believing that I am not enough.
I forgive myself for judging myself as unworthy.
I forgive myself for believing that I'm unlovable.
I forgive myself.
I forgive myself for thinking that somehow I should have done things differently.
I forgive myself for beating myself up over those things.
I've done some things I'm not proud of.
But I did the best I could—
At that time.
Given my circumstances and conditioning.
I forgive myself for believing I should have known better.
I forgive myself for buying into the belief that if I forgive myself, I'm letting myself off the hook and I won't grow and learn from my mistakes.
I forgive myself for believing that I'm not trustworthy.
I forgive myself for judging myself as defective, as lacking, as broken.
I forgive myself for judging myself as stupid, as lazy, as selfish.
I forgive myself for believing that I need to do something in order to be worthy—of love and care.
I forgive myself for believing I have to change myself in order to be acceptable.

I forgive myself for judging myself as a fraud.
I forgive myself for judging myself as inferior, as a loser, as a failure.
I forgive myself for buying into the belief that everyone else is happier, more worthy, confident, and competent than I.
I forgive myself for believing I am not deserving of good things.
I forgive myself for judging myself as bad.
I forgive myself for believing I need to be punished.
I forgive myself for believing the abuse I have suffered was my fault or that I deserved it.
I forgive myself for judging my feelings.
I forgive myself for judging myself as fearful, angry, emotional, aggressive.
I forgive myself for believing my feelings are weak, wrong, too much.
I forgive myself for judging myself as weak.
I forgive myself for believing it is weak to be vulnerable.
I forgive myself for buying into the belief that I need to hide my self and my feelings in order to be safe, accepted.
I forgive myself for believing that I'm helpless.
I forgive myself for believing that I am a victim.
I forgive myself for believing that others are the cause of my upsets.
I forgive myself for believing I need to be fixed or rescued.
I forgive myself for believing I can't handle my problems effectively.
I forgive myself for believing I am my body.
I am more than my body.
I forgive myself for believing I am my feelings.
I am more than my feelings.
I forgive myself for believing I am my thoughts.

I am more than my thoughts.
I forgive myself for believing I am the roles that I play.
I am more than my roles.
I forgive myself for believing I am the things I do.
I am more than my behaviors.
I forgive myself for believing that I am my personality.
I am more than my personality.
All of these aspects change.
My core essence doesn't.
I forgive myself for not seeing that my core essence is good, perfect, and loving—always.

---

## Write Internal Dialogues

Therapeutic writing is one of the most effective healing methods. One of the most powerful approaches is writing an internal dialogue. What you write may resemble a screenplay as you write from your mind to your body or from your body to your mind. You can also write from your heart to your mind and vice versa. It is best to start this kind of writing when you are aware that you have two opposing opinions or feelings about a topic or you are judging yourself for being a certain way.

Rodney chose to write about his on-and-off relationship with his girlfriend using this technique. They had been separated for six months due to her cheating behavior, but in the past, he'd always returned, hoping this time things would be different. He felt conflicted about his feelings toward her and always found himself arguing internally. I encouraged him to write it out instead of just thinking about it. We named the two voices Mind and Heart.

**Mind:** I don't understand why you are still with her. Do you honestly think you can trust her now? She cheated on you three times—at least she *got caught* three times!

**Heart:** I know, but I can see that she loves me. I almost don't take it personally when she cheats. I think she cheats because she is insecure, so it has nothing to do with me. Plus, she knows she is wrong. She is trying to work on it with her therapist. I need her. I enjoy my time with her. I don't like to be alone, on Saturdays especially. We like the same things, and we enjoy each other's company a lot. Besides, no one is perfect.

**Mind:** You are so focused on her and so worried about her behavior that you don't even realize how much you abandon me.

**Heart:** Abandon you?

**Mind:** Yes, abandon me. When you are with her, you don't make time to meditate even though you know how good it feels. You are thinking so much about how she feels that you don't ask me how I feel. This going back and forth, having no stability in the relationship, is draining me. When she cheats, I get obsessed about the details and can't even focus on my work. Then you forgive her, because you feel love for her, and you put me at a risk of being obsessed about her next move. I don't want to think about her anymore.

Rodney came into the session quite shocked as he showed me his journal. He admitted that he'd experienced the most profound insight he'd ever had. He had talked about this issue many times with friends and with past therapists, but writing gave him different access to his true emotions. As he became more aware of his self-damaging behaviors, he decided to make a change in an attempt to reconnect to himself.

## Control Your Thoughts

If you have experienced trauma, not only will your thoughts be negative, but at times you may even have obsessive thoughts. Most of my clients complain about "thinking too much." They often attempt to reduce their thoughts by drinking, doing drugs, overworking, or watching TV excessively. We have a lot on our minds. Our thoughts are not always negative, but having so many of them can be tiring. Most people are more comfortable living in their heads than in their bodies or hearts. You might be thinking of a project you need to complete, the food you need to cook tonight, or the conversation you had with your mother.

Do you know the powerful impact your thoughts can have on you? They can make you depressed, angry, frustrated, lonely, disappointed, fearful, worried, sad, or doubtful. On the other hand, some thoughts can make you smile, make you happy, and help you to relax. The majority of the time, your thoughts directly control how you are feeling at any given moment.

To control your thoughts, you must learn to stop in the middle of them. As you think, simply catch yourself. How often are you occupied by your thoughts? How often are you somewhere other than your physical body because of your thoughts? How are you feeling? What are you thinking about? Of course, controlling your thoughts is much easier said than done. Usually, when we're feeling frustrated, upset, tired, or angry, the tendency is to think about the situation over and over again. We often believe that by thinking about and analyzing the problem, we can solve it. We unconsciously believe that if we think enough about it, we won't have to face our feelings surrounding it. To help keep your thoughts from racing, try the following exercise.

### Exercise 5.3: Five Minutes to Focus

Instead of thinking about whatever is on your mind, take five minutes to focus on being in the here and now. Just look around and try to put your thoughts aside—temporarily. Notice the speed of your thoughts and consciously slow them down. Sit somewhere quiet. Keep your eyes open as you slow your thoughts down. This will be difficult at first; most people spend a good bit of time lost in their thoughts. Focusing on simple things outside in nature can help with this exercise. Notice all the sounds you hear. All of a sudden, you may notice a bird chirping, the cars driving by, or the neighbors laughing. Stay focused on that and nothing else.

Avoid the temptation of trying to make meaning of what you hear or going into memories related to what you hear. Just keep paying attention to the sounds—that is all. In a few minutes, you will notice how your mind slows down and is less focused on other things. If you are noise sensitive and certain noises bother you, you can do the same exercise by focusing on the colors around you instead. Notice all the colors you see. Notice the different shades of yellow, green, and blue, and how many things have different shades. After doing that for a few minutes, notice what happens inside you. You may become aware of an inner quiet compared to how loud it was before.

If you have persistent thoughts that won't leave you alone, write them down. Written down, these thoughts are now outside your mind, and you can get back to them another time. Inside your head, the thoughts have power and seem much larger than they really are.

Another way to control your negative thoughts is by reading inspirational stories or books. This helps replace negative thoughts with positive ones. I often give the analogy of a radio when I talk to clients about how to stop negative thoughts. Imagine that each thought represents a certain channel on a radio. Let's say 97.5 is the thought that says, "You are worthless." When you feel that thought coming over the radio, you switch the channel to, say, 99.5, the one that says, "You are a human being. It is okay to make mistakes." Notice how easy it is to get sucked back into the negative channels. The good news is that you can change the station by becoming aware. Remember that this takes time and practice. Be disciplined. Be your best friend.

## Stay in the Present Moment

I cannot repeat this enough: If you want to heal from your past, you need to stay in the present. During my trauma processing sessions, when clients bring up vivid abuse memories, I remind them gently, "Keep your awareness in the here and now. I know you are talking about what happened when you were five years old, but remember at the same time that it is 2020, and you are in my office now."

I always ask clients to keep their eyes open, especially when they talk about painful memories, to make sure they stay oriented to the room and my presence. Sometimes they say, "But I can really go back into the past better and I feel more of the feelings if I close my eyes."

I tell them, "I know, and I don't want to take your feelings or the memories away. I just don't want you to get overwhelmed, and I don't want you to travel to the past. To heal the past, you have to tolerate being in the present. When these bad things happened to you, you were alone. But I want you to know that now I am here, and I can share your pain as you feel them. Stay here. Stay with me."

Staying in the present moment, or mindfulness as you may have heard it called, is not a new notion. Historically, the arrival of mindfulness in the United States is attributed to Jon Kabat-Zinn, professor of medicine emeritus and creator of the Stress Reduction Clinic at the University of Massachusetts Medical School. He describes mindfulness as awareness that arises through paying attention, on purpose, in the present moment, nonjudgmentally. The practice of mindfulness has now spread around the globe.

Mindfulness can be an important tool in trauma healing, as trauma hijacks the brain. We already have the capacity to be present—mindfulness doesn't require us to change who we are. Mindfulness recognizes and cultivates the best of who we are as human beings. Mindfulness requires practice, but it's easy to learn. You can take mindfulness meditation classes or simply practice it on your own throughout the day.

Influential cultural figures have spoken publicly about their mindfulness practices. Oprah Winfrey swears by mindfulness to help her slow down and appreciate life in the moment, as opposed to scurrying from one thing to the next. LeBron James uses it as mental conditioning so he can perform his best on the basketball court. He even narrates a course on Calm, a meditation app, to help people reach optimal levels of mental fitness. Mindfulness can be beneficial to all people and lifestyles, and there are many ways to go about this practice. Finding the right one for you may involve some trial and error.

Structure is helpful when starting a practice such as mindfulness. Some people establish a daily ritual, which provides a sense of inner order. Morning rituals help establish structure in your daily routine.

When you wake in the morning, notice your thoughts. Are you already anxious about your day? Are you thinking about what happened the day before? Gently bring your thoughts to what you see around you. Feel your face as you wash it with warm water. Notice how the toothbrush feels in your hand. Make your bed mindfully. Being mindful means that you pay attention to what you see: "The sheets are white. I see that they got wrinkled. I am now putting the comforter on top of them."

At first your thoughts will race to where they usually go—to the future or the past, where they are used to hanging out. Don't panic. Don't judge yourself. Gently bring your thoughts back to what you are doing, what you are seeing, and what you are sensing. Do this as much as possible throughout the day. If you are new at this, aim for only about five minutes the first day. Notice the impact on your thoughts for those five minutes. Gradually you can increase the time you spend being mindful.

Phil and I were talking about his alcoholic mother during one of our sessions. As he remembered his mother being in bed most days, he got teary-eyed and more anxious. I noticed right away that his gaze seemed to freeze and he was holding his breath. I verbalized and validated his feelings right away to make him feel safe: "This seems to be a painful memory for you."

He quickly looked away and said, "I'm okay," dismissing his feelings. He was still holding his breath. Children who are neglected often expect not to be taken care of, even as adults. They also believe they have no rights to their feelings, since they had to shut them down to function.

"It is okay to feel this pain now. Feelings are not good or bad. They just are," I added. He briefly made eye contact with me for the first time at this point. I didn't know his capacity to tolerate feelings yet, so I decided to be conservative and not dive into feelings any further. I invited him to bring his awareness to the room instead of his feelings.

"Notice all the colors you see. What gets your attention?"

"I like the painting you have on your wall," he responded.

"What about it?"

"I love the trees. They are very soothing."

After a few more minutes talking about the room, I asked him what he noticed about himself at that moment.

"I am calmer," he said.

"I noticed you are breathing a bit more now," I added. I explained to him that when the right time came, we would explore his feelings and memories, but that for the moment, I wanted to give him the experience of learning to calm his nervous system by simply bringing his attention to the here and now. He was pleasantly surprised. I asked him to practice this skill throughout the week until we met again.

Natalia, a thirty-five-year-old woman, was sitting in my office for the second time after just being released from the hospital. About four years prior, she had come to my treatment center for intensive therapy, but due to financial challenges, she left after two weeks. She reported that the first year following the treatment, she felt much better and stronger emotionally. But as time went by, she forgot to practice the skills she'd learned and life got more and more stressful at home and at work.

Now, just a week before, after battling chronic depression and suicidal thoughts, she had checked herself into the hospital. She didn't want to die, because she loved her children, but she was afraid she would try to kill herself to get rid of the pain she was feeling. During our first meeting, I reminded her of the importance of being present. Within five minutes of starting our meeting, she was already in tears, expressing her fears of feeling her feelings and facing her past trauma.

She had so many thoughts in her head that she didn't even know where to start. The beauty of being in the present is that you learn to reduce your thoughts. You don't go into the past or the future. "I am really scared of talking about my past," she said amid the tears. She was visibly shaking her legs and not making eye contact with me. I assured her that we would only talk about the past when she felt emotionally ready and that she was in charge of the timing.

I asked her to first look around the room and to become aware of her breathing. I said, "You are here now. It is January 2018. You are in my office. I know the feelings are overwhelming. Know that you are safe as you feel them. Just this moment, you are safe. It is okay to feel your feelings. Don't judge yourself. Don't judge the situation. You are okay."

She took a deeper breath organically and said, "I have been angry at myself for feeling this bad." Mindfulness teaches us not to judge anything we feel. Our goal is not to change what is going on but to learn to tolerate what is happening inside us.

I affirmed once again, "Your feelings are okay. You have a right to them, always. You have been in pain for a while. Don't abandon yourself at such a difficult time by judging yourself as bad or wrong. You need *you* now."

She seemed so puzzled at my last statement that she repeated it verbatim: "You need *you*? I never heard that before. I was told, 'Get better—your children need you. Pull yourself together—your husband needs you.' But you are saying I need myself?"

I replied, "Yes, you need to treat yourself in such a way that you can work on your depression and past traumatic memories. You need to stay connected to yourself." Natalia got visibly calmer as our conversation went on like this for the rest of the hour. She let me know that she felt less scared and more present.

To avoid staying in the present moment, people often channel their pain into something else, in both positive and negative ways. People often self-medicate with alcohol or drugs to numb the pain. While this is an unhealthy way to cope, it may keep some people from suicide. Other unhealthy ways of coping include disconnecting from others, perfectionism, over-exercising, love addiction, sex addiction, eating disorders like anorexia, binge eating, and bulimia, and overworking. While these unhealthy coping mechanisms may work in the short term to get someone through something difficult, they don't work in the long term. The good news is that all these unhealthy coping mechanisms can be replaced with healthy ones.

Channeling the pain into something more positive is a healthier way to cope. Some trauma victims make meaning through activism, such as speaking up about rape, making art or writing blogs about their trauma, or volunteering to help other victims. Through these efforts, they work to improve the communities in which they live. They advocate for legal and policy changes to help other victims. Alyssa Milano was one of the first actors to publicly come forward with her story of sexual abuse following the lead of activist Tarana Burke, who started the #MeToo movement. This has encouraged others to come forward with their stories as well.

Finding ways to be in the present moment allows you to become more functional and less symptomatic when dealing with your trauma.

Now that you've learned more about the five different ways to reconnect to your mind, it's time to move on to Step 3, where you reconnect with your body.

## Ten Points to Remember

1. Be aware of how you talk to yourself at all times.
2. Forgive yourself for your past mistakes.
3. Don't talk about traumatic memories without first spending time on building your resources.
4. Let go of your judgments about yourself.
5. Ask others to give you positive feedback.
6. Journal your thoughts and feelings regularly.
7. Spend less time with your thoughts.
8. Spend time doing joyful activities.
9. Be gentle with yourself.
10. Stay in the present and don't go into the future or the past with your thoughts.

"Take care of your body. It's the only place you have to live."

—Jim Rohn

# Step 3

# Reconnect to Your Body

People are not used to thinking of their bodies as part of their emotional well-being. They see their bodies as only physical. They don't see the connection between the body and emotions. But there's a big connection between the two.

When dealing with trauma, recovery happens when you live your life in the present moment. Reconnecting with your body allows you to make this happen. Grounding is one of the best ways to do this. But before you can become grounded, you need to reconnect with your body. For some, coming into the body is painful. That's why reconnecting with your mind (Step 2) is a prerequisite to reconnecting with your body.

CHAPTER 6

# What Does It Mean to Be Disconnected from Your Body?

If you were ever under threat, to deal with the pain and protect yourself, you may have "left your body" by going away into your thoughts. We humans have the capacity to decrease our pain by checking out. Some people even report floating above their bodies, as if they weren't even in them. At a time of great distress, leaving your body may be your only way to survive.

We actually have the capacity to go back into our bodies after the danger is over. But if the danger is constant, this becomes a daunting task, as many of those who were abused as children understand. Even after the danger is over, you may not feel safe coming back to your body. Living outside your body becomes a habit.

In addition, coming back into your body may mean remembering what happened, as you feel the parts of your body associated with the trauma. One client felt neck pain every time we talked about a car accident he'd had a few years before. He had the pain only when he remembered the accident. In psychology this is called dissociation: disconnection or the separation of something from something else, or the state of being disconnected. Dissociation is characterized by a sense of the world as a dreamlike or unreal place and is often accompanied by poor memory of specific events. You may feel foggy while working, have a hard time concentrating, or feel like you can't focus on anything around you.

There is a reason people leave their bodies during or following a traumatic event: to deal with the unbearable pain. This type of natural defense has to be respected. If you're forced to feel your body too soon, you may have a severe reaction. As you continue reading the rest of this chapter, please be respectful of your resistance to feel your body, and do only the exercises that feel good. Remember, not every tool is right for everyone.

Trauma healing occurs when you have new experiences through the body. It requires a change through the physical body first. During the traumatic event, the body reacts a certain way to the incident, and this reaction is stored in the body. When you talk about the traumatic memory, it is crucial that you don't re-create the same reaction in your body. The past lives in us primarily physically and cognitively. That's why we have to change the internal sensations in the body. If we don't, trauma doesn't change and gets repeated over and over again. We have to have new experiences in the body. And we have to learn to become more comfortable with them.

One of my clients disconnected from his body after suffering a serious bike accident. Biking to work was an activity he found joy in, and he looked forward to it every day. When he was hit by a car, he sustained injuries that required hospitalization. After this happened, he felt extremely vulnerable and was terrified of riding his bike again, even after his physical injuries had healed. He no longer felt the joy he once had when riding his bike to work, and this created a sense of loss for him. Our only goal in treatment was to work away the stored trauma he was hanging on to in his body. Once we identified this situation, it took only two sessions of treatment before he felt reconnected to his body and was able to get back on his bike.

Signs of being disconnected from your body might include:

- **Addiction.** There are many types of addiction, but the most detrimental one for trauma healing is substance abuse. If you are using drugs or alcohol to deal with your past, you will have to get sober *before* you can begin to heal your trauma. You will not be able to heal your past if you constantly numb yourself with substances (including marijuana). There are many effective ways to get sober, such as residential or outpatient treatment centers, twelve step meetings with the help of sponsors, and private doctors or therapists. Please seek this help so you can start healing the underlying issues causing you to turn to substances in the first place. Then you can start the larger journey that can change your life. It may be the most important thing you ever do.
- **Self-abandonment.** This includes all the ways you may not be taking care of yourself—not exercising, not eating healthy food, not looking after your personal hygiene, remaining in a toxic work environment even though you could get a better job, being in relationships that are detrimental and abusive, putting other people's needs ahead of your own as if they were more important than you.
- **Dissociation.** This is when your consciousness leaves your body and you feel spacey and disoriented. You may have a conversation but not remember the details. You may take

the wrong exit or not remember how you got to your destination. At work, someone might say, "She was here in the meeting with us, but it was like she wasn't here."

- **Eating Disorders.** People suffering with an eating disorder (ED) often hate their body. They don't like how their body looks, feels, and moves. They see their body as a burden, and their main focus is wanting to change it. They do everything to avoid feeling their body.
- **Chronic Pain.** This could be the result of extreme tension or dissociation from the body.

Instead of disconnecting from your body, try reconnecting with your body through grounding. We'll look into how to do that in the next chapter.

CHAPTER 7

# Coping with Trauma through Grounding

Grounding is a coping strategy designed to immediately connect you with the present moment. Grounding means bringing your attention to your body at the present time. By focusing on your body and what you're physically feeling, you get out of your head, divert your mind from anxious or painful thoughts, and direct your mind into the moment. Grounding techniques are designed to redistribute the focus from your head to your body. Doing so often has an almost instant calming effect.

Grounding techniques are effective not only for trauma processing but also for day-to-day situations. You can even use grounding while you're having a conversation with somebody. You don't need to be in a quiet place or a stressful situation to practice it. In fact, I use it even when I'm waiting for an elevator or driving in my car. When I'm having a conversation with somebody, I give them 90 percent of my attention and I give the other 10 percent to the work of grounding my body.

## A Simple Grounding Activity

Sit comfortably in a chair in an upright position. Make an intention to reduce your thoughts so you can better focus on your senses. Start by looking around the room while breathing normally. Notice what you see: the colors, the shapes, and anything else that gets your attention. Move your neck slowly from right to left, as this helps orient you to your surroundings. Next, pay attention to all the sounds you hear—from loud voices to subtle sounds. You might notice that you were actually not paying attention to the sounds around you at all. Then tune into your sense of smell. Do you pick up any aroma? Are you able to breathe through your nose? Shift your attention now to your sense of taste. What do you notice? Maybe you have just eaten something and you can still taste the food in your mouth. Pay attention to that. Now pay attention to all this at once—what you see, the sounds you hear, the smells you smell, the taste in your mouth. Resist the desire to analyze things. Stay focused on what you perceive instead. Then pause and ask, "How am I feeling?" If you feel uncomfortable, anxious, or scared, stop everything and go back to one of your inner or outer resources (the emotional support tools you identified in Chapter 1). For example, if one of your resources is Disneyland, imagine the positive experience of being there. Don't try to do grounding again today; it is not helpful to push your nervous system. Tomorrow is another day.

However, if you didn't feel uncomfortable after feeling all your senses, the next step is to notice your body. Sit in an upright position and keep your eyes open the whole time. Keep your gaze softly at your knees or your feet. Feel your feet first. Gently push them down to feel them planted on the floor. Then feel your hands as they rest on your knees. How do you feel? Remember that anytime something doesn't feel good, stop what you are doing and go back to the resources you identified in chapter 1—all the techniques you've learned to stabilize yourself.

Next, scan your entire body from head to toe. Stay aware of your breathing. Relax your jaw, your facial muscles, and your throat. Feel your shoulders. Bring them up, first tensing them and then relaxing them and letting their weight go down to your arms. Feel your stomach. Is it tight? Do you feel a certain temperature? Feel your hands and fingers. Do you feel them without moving them? If not, move your fingers slowly. What do you notice? Continue to scan your body in this manner all the way down until you reach your feet. Bring all the weight of your body to your feet. Remember to keep your eyes open, since you need to stay in the here and now. You are more likely to dissociate if you close your eyes.

When you are done with the grounding, again ask yourself how you are feeling. If you notice any negative reaction, stop immediately. If you are feeling calm, stay in this position of noticing your physical sensations. What are you aware of next? Are your thoughts slowing you down? Are you able to stay in this position? Sometimes I hear clients say, "Oh, I'm actually feeling hungry." They didn't *become* hungry in five minutes. They were not even aware that they already *were* hungry. After becoming grounded, they begin to feel their bodies, sometimes for the first time.

I recommend that clients try staying grounded for five minutes while interacting in their day-to-day activities. Pay attention to your body and focus inside your body while you are talking to a coworker, for instance. Do this for about five minutes. What do you notice? If your attention shifts to the person or the outside, bring your attention back into your body and feel your feet on the ground. Be like a detective. Notice everything around you: how the person is talking, how you're feeling, what happens to your thoughts. Then let go of the body focus and just talk normally, without paying attention to anything, and see how that feels. Do you notice any difference? Then try five more minutes of really being in your body and planting your feet firmly on the ground. Center yourself and bring all your attention to the inside of your body. Then jot down all you've noticed.

You can practice grounding when you're stressed or when you find yourself overthinking. You may find yourself ruminating about an upsetting situation or trying to make a decision by going around and around in your thoughts. If you often spend time in your head, you may also be disconnected from your body. Pause for a second, put the thoughts aside, and just get back into feeling physical sensations. Scan your body from head to toe, spend a few minutes doing any of the grounding techniques, and then notice what happens to your thoughts. Do they slow down? Do you feel calmer?

Continue the detective work by noticing when and why you are more likely to check out of your body. Is it when you are stressed or bored or sad or angry? Do you have different reactions with different people? Or in different environments? Notice all these differences. The more you become aware, the more you can stay in your body.

My client Antonio had difficulty relating to this idea of being a detective, so I took him through an exercise. I explained that a detective is someone who pays a lot of attention to every little detail in order to really understand something. The idea is to increase awareness in the body. Awareness is the first step to staying grounded and present.

Antonio was a very successful businessman who was used to handling all kinds of difficult business decisions. When I asked him how he felt, he responded, "Sad."

I shared, "That feeling of sadness is in your body. Notice your body when you are talking about being sad."

"Guys aren't supposed to be sad," he said.

"That's a thought, not a feeling. What happens in your body when you feel sad?"

"I feel angry."

"What sensation do you feel when you are angry? What part of your body feels the anger?"

"It feels like my stomach is tied up in knots. My jaw gets tight. My hands tighten up and I make a fist."

Now Antonio was actually connecting the feeling of anger to his body and noting the sensation of anger in his body. That's the goal. Pay attention to how your body is reacting to a feeling.

When you say things like, "I feel sad," "I feel happy," or "I feel numb," see how your body reacts. It can provide you with a lot of information. By doing the detective work of digging deeper, you can explore how your body reacts to these feelings.

## Why Is Grounding Important?

When trauma happens, you may leave your physical body in order to deal with the physical or emotional pain. This is why it's crucial that you stay in your body when you work on trauma memories to heal the past. A lot of people skip this important step in trauma healing. This was the case when Sheila came to see me for the first time after a negative experience with her previous therapist. In their second session, the therapist decided that Sheila was ready to work on her past memory of being abandoned by her mother. The therapist encouraged Sheila to go straight into the memory of when she was seven years old without doing much preparation work of grounding and resourcing.

Much to her surprise, Sheila found herself in tears and almost panicked. She described the rest of the hour as an awful experience.

She was shaking and crying as her therapist kept encouraging her to continue to process the memories. This was too soon too fast for Sheila because she hadn't built in any resources or done any grounding exercises to stay connected to her body. At the end of the session, the therapist realized that Sheila was quite dysregulated, but there wasn't enough time left to help calm her nervous system.

Sheila decided not to go back to therapy and didn't seek any help for another year. Then one of her best friends, whom I was working with, encouraged her to try trauma therapy again. She reluctantly walked through the doors of the Reconnect Treatment Center.

When I met Sheila, I could see that she was terrified of feeling her body and that it would take a long time before I could gain her trust and create the safety in her body that she had abandoned. I spent the first couple of sessions educating Sheila about how I do trauma therapy. She was quite surprised to hear about the importance of including the body in her healing. She realized that she had been disconnected from her body ever since she was a little girl. We spent the following sessions resourcing and grounding, and I gave her other tools to help calm her nervous system.

Research on grounding has been emerging in the twenty-first century. It's still in its infancy, but the results are promising. The studies are all encouraging, but you don't need external scientific evidence. Just practice the techniques and evaluate the results for yourself. Grounding reduces stress, reduces inflammation, improves the immune system, elevates mood, and improves blood flow. The more rooted you are in your body, the less stress and anxiety you experience.

CHAPTER 8

# Our Bodies Remember Even When Our Minds Don't

Reconnecting with your body has to happen in a slow and gentle way. Exercise is one way to reconnect. My client Jess, however, had a hard time doing physical exercises. Each time she did, she had flashbacks of past sexual abuse. We had to limit how much she exercised and gradually build on it.

Sometimes touching the body in an area that has been hurt can trigger memories in an overwhelming way. One of my clients quit seeing a therapist who insisted on doing "touch work" at their second meeting. Apparently the therapist, upon finding out that the client had a severe history of childhood neglect and not being loved, decided that she needed to be touched because she was lacking her mother's affection. The client lay on a massage table while the therapist touched her body to regulate her nervous system. This technique, although effective with some people, proved to be the wrong treatment. The client went into a panic attack when the therapist touched her because she was not ready for such an encounter.

Some rape survivors claim to hate their bodies because of what happened to them. I tell them, "Your body's not the one who abused you. It's the perpetrator who did it. Your body is just a messenger of the pain. So if you continue to believe that it's your body's fault, then you're not going to want to be in your body. It's not your body's fault."

The body stores memories even when the mind doesn't remember an event. Making peace with your body must be gradual—especially if you are a sexual abuse survivor. Even pleasant activities can often be negative triggers. Before you can do exercises to feel your body, you have to make sure this kind of work is tolerable for you. Trauma happened in the past. That is why trauma survivors feel stuck in the past and often have a hard time staying in the present. This is why I suggest first working on reconnecting to your mind.

## Healing Trauma without Talking about It

A resource, by definition, is a source of supply or support, especially one that can be readily drawn upon when needed. Many patients, such as Gail, are apprehensive to talk about their trauma right away. They tell me something along the lines of, "I thought I would have to tell you what happened to me, with all the details, to get it off my chest. But every time I try that, I get panicky. First my heart races. Then I get nauseated and feel dizzy. I will never be able to heal this trauma." I assure them that there is another way to work around this issue. This is when I introduce the need for resources that one can turn to. The following exercise explores ways to feel safe.

## Exercise 8.1: Ways to Feel Safe

Think of all the things and people that make you feel good, relaxed, or safe. The list might include a pet, your grandmother, Disneyland, the ocean, the mountains, trees, Mother Mary, or your favorite movie.

Take a look at each item one at a time. If your list includes Disneyland, for instance, write a description of what you like about this place. Writing as opposed to only thinking about it makes the experience stronger. If negative thoughts sneak in while you are doing this exercise, skip this item and go to another one.

Again using the example of Disneyland, imagine being there. What is the weather like? What do you see? What is your favorite ride? Imagine walking around and looking at other people. Do they seem happy? How do you feel? Notice the good feeling you have and locate that feeling in your body. Is your heart warm? Are your shoulders relaxed? Stay with the positive sensations in your body while imagining strolling around Disneyland. If you want, write about the sensations.

The key in this exercise is to stay in the positive feeling and the positive sensation in your body as long as you can. Once you are done with one item in your list, do the same thing with the other items. Keep these resources handy. Consider them your internal support system for any stressful situations you may encounter throughout the day.

## It Works

Over the years, I have worked with a number of veterans who were sexually abused during their military service. I created a fourteen-day intensive treatment for six survivors at a time and ran it with other therapists. During the fourteen days, we practiced grounding techniques a few times every day, in addition to other trauma treatment techniques. At the end of the program, the survivors shared that for the first time in years, they were finally feeling themselves in their bodies, feeling themselves as whole. Some of them had suffered with the symptoms of trauma for decades and had lost hope. They also realized that the anger they were feeling toward their perpetrators had never been expressed or acknowledged properly, so the anger had turned inward. In some cases, they had turned the anger toward their bodies indirectly by overeating or using drugs. Some had tried counseling but felt no relief, because the treatment did not include the body as part of the healing. They had told their stories in group settings, but their bodies still suffered with the pain and the memories. A couple of the survivors had even developed chronic pain with no physical reason behind it. As they started experiencing their bodies day after day, they felt a sense of peace and compassion toward themselves. With the right support, they were able to reconnect to their bodies.

## Grounding on the Move

There are many simple ways to connect with your body. If you find sitting down and concentrating on your senses too difficult, try to do it during a walk. If you live by the beach or another natural setting, practice grounding while moving in this environment. Take your shoes off and walk barefoot on the beach or the grass. Feel the warmth of the sun on your skin. Listen to the rhythm of the crashing waves or the wind. Smell the ocean wind as it brushes past you. Now notice your feet. Do you feel a tingly sensation in your feet or legs as warmth rises up your body? Notice your whole body now. Do you feel the sand, the little rocks, or the wet grass? Feel and stay connected to the earth. Expand the good feeling throughout your body. The following exercise will help when you are anxiety-stricken.

## Exercise 8.2: Rapid Ways to Ground in a Moment of Anxiety

Try one of the following grounding techniques right now to observe the effects or to remember in case of an emergency. They each take a few seconds, and you can practice them any time.

1. **When you are ungrounded, place one hand over the top of your head.** Gently push your hand down and feel the weight of your head go down to your feet. Keep your eyes open.
2. **Stand with your feet parallel to one another, at least as far apart as your shoulders.** Plant your feet as firmly as possible on the ground. Keep your head straight, chin tucked, and spine straight. Rest your hands at your side. Let all your body's weight and tension go into your feet, allowing them to be absorbed into the ground. To support this grounding process, imagine roots growing out the bottom of your feet, like the roots of a tree, extending deep into the ground beneath you.
3. **Feel your nose as the air enters and goes out.** Feel your lungs as they move during breathing. Inhale for three

seconds and then exhale for five seconds or more, until your lungs are empty.

4. **Take a cold shower.** If you're not accustomed to cold showers, start with a hot shower. At the end, for thirty seconds, gradually turn the water slightly cooler until it's cold. By the end of three weeks, your body will be used to the cold temperature. While you are under the water, feel it against your skin. Don't do this if you have high blood pressure.
5. **Roll around like a cat.** Have you ever noticed how cats and some dogs roll around on the ground? Try rolling around and getting dirty. Feel the joy of it.

---

## Emotional Freedom Technique

According to Gary Craig, developer of the emotional freedom technique (EFT), tapping on different parts of the body helps to balance energy and reduce physical and emotional pain. You can use EFT when you are upset or during trauma processing sessions with your therapist. You can use EFT as a stand-alone tool or in conjunction with therapy or other techniques. It takes just a few minutes and helps you feel calmer right away. The following exercise helps you practice EFT.

### Exercise 8.3: Working on Your Feelings

Determine what feeling you would like to work on. Let's start with anxiety.

Rate the feeling from 0 to 10, with 10 being the worst.

Tap the karate chop point (the center of the fleshy part of the outer hand) with your other hand while saying, "Even though I feel anxious, I still love and accept myself." Do this three times.

Then tap the following points seven to ten times. Each time, repeat the negative feeling you are trying to change.

- Between the two eyebrows: "This anxiety"
- Side of the eye: "This anxiety"
- Under the eye: "This anxiety"
- Under the nose: "This anxiety"
- The chin: "This anxiety"
- Under the collarbone: "This anxiety"
- Under the armpit: "This anxiety"
- Top of the head: "This anxiety"

Repeat the tapping exercise at least twice. Then take a deep breath and settle in your body. Now rate the disturbing feeling again, from 0 to 10. Repeat the tapping until the feeling decreases to a tolerable rate. Sometimes the feeling may change. For instance, once the anxiety is relieved, sadness may come up. If this happens, repeat the tapping routine using the feeling of sadness instead of anxiety.

---

## The Body Knows—How It Can Help with Decision Making

When making a big decision, people often write lists of pros and cons, but they neglect to allow the body to have a say in the decision. My client Jody was wrestling with a big decision: where to move. She was considering three different states: Montana, Washington, and New York. I asked her to write the place-names on a piece of paper. I then asked her about each state. I said, "Now I'm going to ask you to think about Montana. Don't tell me your thoughts, but tell me exactly what happens in your body." She responded, "My body feels tired and my stomach feels tight."

"Okay, take a deep breath and let it go. Now think of Washington. What is happening in your body now?" I asked.

"It's strange. My shoulders are relaxing," she said. Finally I asked her about New York. Her body once again felt tense. Eventually, she chose to move to Washington because her body agreed with her. Her body made her decision making so much easier. Pros/cons lists can still be helpful, but when you create a separate list of how your body responds, it provides you with more information. People often refer to this as listening to your gut.

Use your body as a resource. Unfortunately, when people are traumatized, they often don't see the body as a resource. Instead they view it as a reminder of a painful memory. So they leave their bodies. Once they begin feeling calmer and are more willing to come back to their bodies, they realize that the trauma is not happening today. It truly is in the past. That's when the real healing begins. The body talks. You are doing a huge disservice to yourself if you don't listen to it. To listen to your body, treat it with respect, starting with something as simple as your posture.

## Your Posture Affects How you Feel

Poor posture can put you in a lousy mood and make you feel more stressed and depressed. Poor posture does not directly cause serious problems like clinical depression and anxiety, but it may exacerbate the symptoms of these disorders. In my practice I have observed many times the connection between poor posture and fatigue, especially in people who have depression. Most people with mild depression feel more alert and centered by simply keeping their backs and shoulders upright while sitting. When they shift to a more upright position, their outlook and energy levels increase. They also report less anxiety.

## Exercise 8.4: The Effects of Posture on Your Emotions

Put your head down and say, "I am happy." What do you notice? Do you really feel happy and upbeat in that posture?

Now sit upright and hold your head in an upright position as well. Say, "I am sad." What do you notice now? Most people tell me it is hard to feel sad with the body in this upright position.

---

Forty-five-year-old Julie came to see me for a few months after separating from her husband of twenty-five years. As time went by, her husband became more and more aggressive and greedy. Through therapy, Julie started remembering childhood abuse by her father that resembled her husband's behavior. She got increasingly overwhelmed and severely dissociated after each conversation with her husband.

One afternoon she came in almost in tears and wondered if she should pause the divorce proceedings. "What happens in your body as you say that?" I asked her. As if she didn't hear me, she started telling me about how she attempted suicide when she was thirteen. I repeated the question—still no direct response. I realized then that her voice had changed and sounded like a little girl's. Her body posture was slumped. She leaned backward, with her eyes looking up and her legs crossed tightly. It was obvious that she was dissociating by regressing in age, and my goal was to bring her attention back to the here and now.

I could have taken the opportunity to help her process this earlier memory, but to tolerate feelings from the past, you have to have a solid ground in the here and now first. I had to be very careful not to go down the rabbit hole of the story, otherwise she was going to stay in the state of a thirteen-year-old. I asked her to explain what was happening with her legs. "I cross them like a pretzel," she said, almost in a whispering voice. She giggled like a young girl as she told me she had always been very flexible and that crossing her legs made her feel good. I was now able to talk about her body without adding more stress to her overwhelmed feelings. I asked her to keep her awareness of the good sensation of her legs as she told me the rest of what she wanted to share.

Julie said, "When I was a child, I took a bunch of pills one day to kill myself. My parents called the paramedics and the firemen showed up at my house. I will never forget—one of them made eye contact with me and asked why I wanted to die. I told him, 'No one likes me.' He kept his soft and gentle eyes on me and said, 'When you grow up, you will realize a lot of people like you.'" She burst into tears as she said that.

I asked, "Was the fireman right?" She smiled. "Yes, he was right. There are many people who like me." She put her hand on her heart as she took a deep breath. I guided her further into feeling her body. "Feel the warmth of your own hand and notice what happens in your body next." She sat a bit more upright. I directed her to uncross her legs, press both feet on the ground, and sit up straighter. "Now how do you feel?"

"Much better, actually," she claimed.

"Did you notice your voice changed?" Her giggly teenage voice had changed into an adult voice again.

Many factors helped Julie: remembering a positive experience, being able to soothe herself by placing her hand on her heart, sitting upright with her feet on the ground, and the memory of being cared about by the fireman. I grounded this experience with her by reminding her that she could calm herself when she was alone and felt sad.

## Ways to Love and Connect to Your Body

Just like Julie, traumatized people need to have physical and sensory experiences to unlock their bodies, to activate the fight-or-flight response, to tolerate their sensations, to befriend their inner experiences, and to cultivate new action patterns. The following list includes different ways to connect to your body:

- Yoga
- Somatic therapies
- Taking care of your physical health
- Not using drugs or alcohol to numb your pain
- Eating in a healthy way
- Exercising
- Effective action (such as boxing or martial arts)
- Tai chi
- Mindful meditation
- Dance
- Singing in a choir
- Playing sports

I watched Julie closely and happily as she went from being a pale, quiet, and sad woman to being the happy, funny, and vibrant person she always knew she was. Most importantly, she began sculpting again. This didn't happen in one day—it happened over time. As her mood lifted, she started talking joyfully about her art and eventually wanting to pick it up again. This was the most amazing moment for me as a psychologist. Julie was connecting to herself through her joy in making art.

For some, physical exercise doesn't work. My client Amber tried running on a treadmill to release her tremendous anxiety. She had been severely physically abused as a child. She knew physical exercise was good for her but simply couldn't tolerate it. The rapid heartbeats brought on more anxiety. For Amber, it was more beneficial to do muscle-building exercises. Building muscles made her feel more emotionally contained and more grounded.

However you choose to reconnect with your body, listen to your body. It's not a one-size-fits-all mentality. Do what feels best at the time, be patient with yourself, and stay in the here and now.

## Ten Points to Remember

1. Be gentle with yourself.
2. Make peace with your body.
3. Orient yourself to the present moment by focusing on your bodily sensations.
4. Incorporate daily grounding practice.
5. Remember that practicing self-discipline is practicing self-love.
6. Eat healthy and nutritious food.
7. Exercise.
8. Watch your addictive behaviors.
9. Surround yourself with supportive people.
10. Practice yoga.

"We cannot be more sensitive to pleasure without being more sensitive to pain."

—Alan Watts

# Step 4

# Reconnect to Your Heart

Left alone—traumatized and neglected—a person can become overwhelmed and organize life around not feeling. As a result, life is essentially robbed of pleasure and vitality.

When we experience trauma, we go through unbearable feelings of pain, sadness, anger, shame, isolation, grief, and loss. The pain can be so intense at the time of the incident that we feel like we will die if we allow the feelings ever to be present again. Especially for children, the fear of dying from these intense feelings is very strong and real. Human beings have a great innate ability to shut down feelings as a defense mechanism, which is evident in children. Often the closest adults are the same people who hurt us, so we don't have anyone to turn to for comfort. Many people with trauma try to escape their emotions. This is called avoidance. It comes in handy when dealing with uncomfortable thoughts, feelings, or conversations about the traumatic event, and that places and people that remind you of the event. Having trouble remembering parts of a traumatic event is also part of avoidance. Avoidance helps us run away from uncomfortable emotions like fear, sadness, or shame. This is how we survive.

Emotional avoidance may be effective in the short run and provide some temporary relief. However, in the long run, the emotions you try to avoid may actually grow stronger.

CHAPTER 9

# Why Emotional Avoidance Does Not Work

Emotional avoidance is often considered, in the long run, an unhealthy coping strategy. We have emotions for a reason. Emotions provide us with information about ourselves and the things going on around us. For example, the emotion of fear tells us we may be in danger. The emotion of sadness tells us we may need some time to take care of ourselves or seek comfort from others. Given the important role they play in our lives, our emotions are there to be experienced, and they eventually *need* to be experienced.

Although we characterize it as an unhealthy coping strategy, keep in mind that emotional avoidance is necessary sometimes. And it can be very effective as long as it doesn't become a chronic problem. For instance, in the case of an emergency, you might have to avoid pain to survive. If you have a horrific car accident, you can't afford to panic, because if you panic you might not be able to get out of the car or dial 911 for help. So at this point, emotional avoidance is a good thing. However, it's not good if after the emergency passes, you're still saying, "Oh, I'm fine. It's no problem that I had a car accident and broke my legs. I'm tough." The reality is, if you try to push the pain aside, it sneaks up on you eventually in different ways. Emotional avoidance served you well right after the car accident, because it shut down your emotions and didn't send you into a panic, but it does not serve you well later.

When you shut down feelings, you run the risk of shutting down *all* feelings—including happiness and joy. My client Veronica's childhood was full of traumas. She had difficulty talking about her childhood. As we began working together and she shared some of those memories, something unexpected happened. All of a sudden, she had a positive memory about her childhood. She remembered her father spending quality time with her on a vacation. She burst into tears, recognizing that her childhood wasn't just about negative experiences. There were some good moments in there too. By shutting out her entire childhood, she wasn't able to see some of the happiness and joy that was also part of her childhood. Now she was able to see both sides.

It is human nature to have feelings, and we should embrace them all without judging whether they are bad or good. We experience all kinds of feelings. We don't only have happiness. We don't only have joy. It's easy to label feelings as good or bad, but it's not necessary to do that. Sure, we don't want to be sad all the time, but we need to understand and accept the polarity between happy and sad. If you cut off the negative feelings, eventually your nervous system may not know how to differentiate between negative and positive feelings. Before you know it, you might fully disconnect from all feelings, ending up numb and without joy.

Avoiding emotions also takes considerable effort, especially when those emotions are strong. We think we can push them away, but in fact they only go down, not away. As avoided emotions pile up and become stronger, more and more effort is needed to keep them at bay. As a result, little energy may be left for the important things in your life, such as family and friends. In addition, at any unexpected moment, all repressed emotions can surface and create chaos for you. Using all your energy to avoid certain emotions may make it difficult to manage other experiences, such as frustration and irritation, making you more likely to be on edge and angry.

If you try to shut down your feelings, they may "fight back" so they can be experienced and listened to. If you are determined to avoid your emotions, you might turn to more drastic and unhealthy approaches, such as substance abuse. You might become addicted to alcohol, drugs, food, sex, gambling, or even exercise. These substances and activities are only filling the void so that you don't have to deal with your feelings.

Another way to avoid negative feelings is through fantasy. When we are young, we have a great capacity for fantasy. Fantasy becomes a rescuer in many situations. Children might go far into fantasy worlds to run away from painful feelings. They may continue this habit as adults. Adults fantasize about having whatever they missed as children—mostly the perfect family. My client Colleen lived a fantasy life because of a past trauma. She first came to see me at age forty-six due to her relationship challenges. She regularly fell in love with someone new and exciting. The days she was "in love," she seemed happy, giggly, not minding any other stress, and feeling strong and valued. However, when any small problem within the relationship showed up, her mood would crash and she'd become depressed. Her mood swings became unbearable. That is why she came to therapy.

I gathered a lot of information about her childhood to make sense of her reactions and to educate her about her patterns. She grew up with an abusive father who often beat up her mother and was emotionally absent from his children. Colleen loved her father and desperately tried to have a relationship with him. Her mother, who was a master at hiding feelings and pretending everything was fine, was not a good role model for Colleen. When she was thirteen, her father died suddenly from colon cancer. Colleen's mother simultaneously felt relief and agony at losing her husband. Colleen remembers feeling confused about her own grief as well.

Around age fifteen, she started dating and noticed that she had angry outbursts if she felt boys were rejecting her. When she was twenty, she met a young, handsome, and charming guy at her cousin's wedding in France. She fell in love immediately and got married only three months later. She felt as if her dreams had come true: living in France, having her own family. She got pregnant right away, and the abuse started during pregnancy. Unfortunately, she stayed in this abusive relationship for fifteen years. When I met her, she had finally divorced.

One month into our work together, she "fell in love" with a professor at the school where she was working on her master's degree. As usual, she was glowingly talking about him. They had met only once, for coffee, but she was convinced he was the man she had been waiting for. She was already so obsessed with him that she couldn't sleep well at night and couldn't concentrate on her schoolwork. She didn't know why she was so desperately seeking to fall in love. She didn't realize that it had to do with the grief she felt from her failed marriage and her failed childhood family unit. For Colleen, love addiction was a way to fill the void left by an abusive childhood and marriage. She was trying to reconnect to her heart and feelings but didn't know how.

Colleen's story demonstrates why it's not healthy to use emotional avoidance techniques that disconnect you from your heart. In the next chapter, you'll learn how to tell if you are disconnected from your heart. But before doing that, let's look at the messages you received as a child.

## Exercise 9.1: Childhood Messages

Write down what messages about emotions you received as a child. These are your core beliefs. What did you learn from family, school, or church? Read the list and see if you have more to add, since over the years you might have experienced painful events that taught you different lessons. Maybe when you first broke up with a girlfriend or boyfriend, you thought, "Loving is not good." Or maybe, if your parents hit you because you were crying, you learned that "crying means danger," and you learned to stop the tears. In the first column, share what you learned. In the second column, write down how you would like to change that thought.

| What I learned | What I wish I learned |
|---|---|
| | |
| | |
| | |

John, a forty-year-old, came to my center to deal with his past trauma of sexual and physical abuse. He reported that recently he'd had memories of early abuse after being fired from a job he loved. As he was talking about some of the past abuse, I noticed that his voice was really low, his jaw was tight, and he was holding his breath. When I asked him to do the same exercise, here is what he came up with.

| What I learned | What I wish I learned |
| --- | --- |
| Anger means violence | It is okay to be angry |
| Be quiet if you don't want to be hit | I have a right to talk |
| Don't ask anything | It is okay for me to ask for what I want |
| Sadness is for weak people | It is okay for me to feel sad |
| It is better to think than feel | Feelings are okay too |

CHAPTER 10

# How Do You Know If You Are Disconnected from Your Heart and Feelings?

Before we look at signs that you are disconnected from your heart and feelings, know that if you are, you most likely disconnected to protect yourself. Don't judge yourself for this. Instead, show empathy for protecting yourself when it was necessary in the past. Not sure if you are disconnected from your heart and feelings? The following list of symptoms may help you recognize if you are:

- **Feeling numb.** This is a chronic sense of feeling blah. It's difficult for you to enjoy things you used to enjoy.
- **Depression.** Depression is a chronic sense of feeling low. Often, it's not related to daily issues but is an overall sense of regularly feeling sad or hopeless. You may find it difficult to do daily chores and tasks.

- **Anger management issues.** If you cut off your feelings, they can pile up and express themselves as anger. If you have a hard time managing your anger or have been told you have a short fuse, you may have other feelings underneath the anger. Many people are more comfortable feeling their anger than their sadness.
- **Feeling confused.** This is when you can't label your feelings anymore. The feelings have been piling up for so long that you can't even differentiate anger from sadness.
- **Loss of intuition.** This is your gut sense. If you are traumatized, you may not be able to have a gut sense about people or things, or you may hear your intuition but no longer follow it. You don't trust your own instincts. In other words, you may not be able to follow your heart.
- **Love addiction.** If you didn't form a healthy relationship with your parents, you may find yourself in search of this love in another person on an ongoing basis. People with a love addiction are often in love with the feeling of being in love, which triggers compulsive behavior. They are constantly looking to be in love so they don't have to experience feelings they have been avoiding—probably all their lives.
- **Feeling disconnected from others.** This is manifested as having difficulty forming loving relationships due to a fear of being hurt. You may reject others or perceive that others reject or abandon you.
- **Physical illness.** The American Psychological Association tells us that prolonged stress can contribute to heart disease. The way we respond to stress can make just as much of an impact on the heart as smoking. Studies show that happier people have healthier levels of fibrinogen and cortisol in their blood, making them less susceptible to heart disease.

> People with depression are twice as likely to develop cardiovascular issues.

What price are you willing to pay to not reconnect to your heart? Sad and angry feelings can provide valuable lessons and opportunities for healing. Award-winning author and poet Vironika Tugaleva once said, "The most profound personal growth does not happen while reading a book or meditating on a mat. It happens in the throes of conflict—when you are angry, afraid, frustrated."

When we are sad or angry, it's natural to want to escape these feelings. One of my clients, Brad, used marijuana to help mellow him out. He told me, "When I smoke pot, I actually feel more grounded. I feel much more relaxed and feel good." He didn't see the harm in it. I told him, "That is because you are high. That's why you are relaxed. You are smoking pot to feel good, but you aren't dealing with your real feelings. You are doing this to avoid your feelings. While it may seem like a good idea in the short term and bring you happiness, there's a flip side you need to realize. There's a price tag for not dealing with your feelings. You're not seeing the big picture."

## We Need to Feel Our Feelings

Unfortunately, there is no such thing as getting rid of feelings. They can't be pushed away—only pushed down. In order to heal, we need to feel our feelings again. Feelings should be felt without judgment and fear. We need to not label feelings as "good" or "bad." In fact, this attitude toward feelings is very Western. Many Eastern philosophies, such as Buddhism, accept feelings as they are and teach that *all* feelings are necessary and complementary. To deny a feeling means denying who you are; to cut off a feeling means cutting off a part of yourself.

People tell me that I'm very transparent with my emotions. I've had people say, "You're a psychologist. Why are you angry?" They have this idea that psychologists should not show emotions like anger. That couldn't be further from the truth.

Accept that we are fragile beings and that we get hurt. Human beings fantasize about being perfect and not being impacted by negative incidents. People get really upset that trauma leaves them with scars. We look desperately for answers and healing magical powers to get rid of our trauma once and for all. We hate ourselves when we realize we are still carrying the trauma inside.

When I learned to deal with my own emotions, I noticed the same old unhealthy voice saying, "You can't deal with feelings; you can't tolerate them. Sadness is bad. Happiness is good." I was very uncomfortable having feelings. Instead, I felt "strong" in my thoughts and actions. I trusted my mind but not my heart.

I decided to challenge the old unhealthy voice. So I started saying over and over again, "I can tolerate feelings. I will not die. I can take it. I am stronger now." Today, I still use self-talk daily. I am my best friend at that moment. I must admit that I am at an advantage, since my job is to encourage people and help them overcome fears and trauma. When my own trauma gets triggered, I imagine I am a client and I have a dialogue with myself, the therapist. I am not "faking it till I make it." I genuinely believe we are more resourceful than we think—I witness that every day with my clients. My empathy toward *them* helps me be more empathic and gentler with *myself*. I like to remember what Confucius said: "It does not matter how slowly you go as long as you do not stop."

CHAPTER 11

# Reconnecting the Dots

As you continue to heal from your trauma and reconnect with your heart, there are things you can do to help with these goals. Everyone is different, so some of the tools might not feel right to you while others may resonate with you. I encourage you to at least consider what I'm about to share and try it out. These tools are easy to implement, and I use them myself. I've been journaling almost daily since I was twelve or thirteen. Writing in my journal is the best therapeutic method for me. I like to do it right away in the morning. It's part of my regular morning routine.

## Daily Journaling

James Pennebaker, a University of Texas–Austin psychologist and researcher, has shown that regular journaling has a positive impact on well-being, even strengthening immune cells. Pennebaker believes that writing about stressful events helps you come to terms with them, acting as a stress management tool, thus reducing the impact of stressors on your physical health.[14]

Writing about your feelings daily in your journal is an essential step in healing. When you talk about what happened to you, you access the frontal cortex (rational brain) versus the more emotional brain. However, feelings are stored in the emotional side of the brain. We access that side of the brain through writing, music, and art.

Every morning when you wake up, write at least three pages of thoughts and feelings in a free-form style. Write nonstop without thinking. Write whatever comes to your mind, and if nothing comes to your mind, feel free to write, "I don't know what to write. This is stupid. I don't feel anything." You will be surprised how you start getting in touch with your feelings as you do daily writings this way. Some people prefer a journal with prompts—statements that prompt you to write something.

I gave Colleen "journal your feelings" homework to help her with her love addiction. She was strongly caught up in her addiction as she obsessively thought about her "Prince Charming." She wrote about her feelings on the following questions: "What will I think about if I don't think about him? What do I feel underneath this obsession?" Addictive behaviors are often there because they mask deeper feelings, such as sadness and grief. I also asked her to write the answer to these questions: "What do I feel sad about? And what does that remind me of?"

Another helpful exercise is to write about feelings that you usually avoid. Every day in your journaling, set aside some time to write about sadness and anger that you may have pushed away. Most people try to push away feelings for years. I recommend

---

[14] Maud Purcell, "The Health Benefits of Journaling," Psych Central, 2020, https://psychcentral.com/lib/the-health-benefits-of-journaling, accessed September 2, 2020.

allowing yourself to feel these negative feelings daily, even if you think you have nothing to be sad or angry about. Experiment with that for a whole month. Write about current or past issues that make you feel sad or bad to increase your tolerance for negative feelings and to reduce the accumulation of repressed feelings. You may be quite surprised at the outcome. Please be gentle with the writing, however, since feelings can overwhelm you. If you have been avoiding your emotions for a long time, it may be difficult to release them. Sometimes, when we let emotions build up, they escape all at once. This may lead to emotions feeling out of control. As you begin reconnecting to your feelings, realize that it takes time and practice to do so.

## Mindfulness—Sitting with Emotions

The more we can meet any difficulty with presence, compassion, and kindness, the easier we can move through it. Feelings can't hurt us. They are felt in the body, and the most difficult emotional pain is minor when it comes to its physical sensation.

## Exercise 11.1: Practicing Mindfulness

1. Think of a current situation that evokes negative feelings. It should not be a serious situation. You should not rate these feelings higher than 5 out of 10 (with 10 being the worst).
2. Notice your body. Where in your body are you feeling the sensations?
3. What are your thoughts about this situation?
4. How do you feel? Do you say, "I can't stand feeling this way" or "It isn't right that I feel so bad"?

Often, people feel anger when they feel sad or vulnerable, thereby increasing the intensity of the initial negative feelings. Mindfulness practice encourages you to "sit with" these strong emotions and observe them as they ebb and flow in your body. All emotions will come and go if we let them. Once the emotion has softened, you can think of ways you want to respond (or not) to the situation.

---

## Positive Distraction

If your emotions feel too strong, try positive distraction instead of avoidance. Do something to temporarily distract you from a strong emotion, such as reading a book, calling a friend, or being out in nature. Consider taking an Epsom salt bath to help relax muscles and loosen joints. You may choose to make this part of your regular self-care routine. Any of these positive distractions can give emotions time to decrease in strength, making it easier to cope with them.

There's a difference between positive distraction and just being distracted. If you are using distraction to avoid feelings, that can be dangerous. You may be overwhelmed by your feelings and tell yourself, "I'm going to watch TV tonight because I want to veg out. I don't want to ever think about what happened today." That's an unhealthy avoidance behavior, and it has nothing to do with watching TV. In contrast, if you feel overwhelmed by your feelings and tell yourself, "I am having a difficult time right now dealing with my feelings. I will deal with them tomorrow. But tonight, I will take a nice bath and then watch a little TV to veg out," you are using the television as a positive distraction instead of avoiding your feelings altogether. Then, tomorrow, when you wake up, you can go back to dealing with your feelings. If you wake up and choose to forget those feelings of yesterday, they might catch up with you when you least expect it. The "empty chair" technique is a great way to deal with those feelings.

## The Empty Chair Technique

My client Manuela learned to make peace with her feelings during our therapy sessions. In one session she said she was feeling an internal conflict about her emotions. She was feeling angry at herself for not being able to tolerate her sadness. She judged herself as weak and didn't know how to overcome this fear of her feelings. Whenever a client expresses a conflict inside, it is my first priority to work that conflict out, since the most important relationship is the one with yourself.

To help her gain clarity, I offered the well-known gestalt empty chair technique. We put two chairs facing each other, and I moved into a third chair as "the neutral observer." I explained the process to her: "In one chair, we will put the part of you that feels shut down and can't feel, and the other one will hold the part of you that is angry about this. You will then go back and forth between the chairs and have a dialogue. I am merely a guide in this process. You will talk to each other, not to me."

She started first with the part that was angry: "You don't let me feel. You made me have half of a life. I need to feel, but you don't allow me." She complained in an angry tone to the part of her she called "fear of feelings." She then got up and sat in the other chair. Her demeanor changed almost instantly. "Fear" responded, "I am too scared to open up. I am afraid I might die, or others may get angry at me. Please don't be mad at me. I don't want to talk about how I feel. I have to always pretend like nothing is wrong. I can't show feelings. I have to protect myself from predators. You want me to be ready for you, but I am not." Manuela seemed surprised to hear that. She was able to show some empathy toward herself for the first time. "I feel your pain. I thought you were dead inside, but actually you are scared," she said from the anger chair.

"Fear" continued the dialogue: "I am so glad to see that you accept me. I have been cold and lonely inside." This conversation went on for about half an hour, with Manuela moving back and forth between the chairs. At the end she was in tears and expressed feeling much more peace than ever before about this topic. She also remembered that her mother had never tolerated her feelings. In fact, Manuela was punished if she got angry or sad.

Reva, age thirty six, grew up in a physically abusive household. When she first came to me, she often had nightmares about her father yelling at her and beating her up severely. He had broken her bones many times. Reva and I, after completing the stabilization phase, started working on the memories of this physical torture. Through many hard sessions and tears, Reva started feeling stronger and her nightmares decreased significantly. She wanted to do more therapeutic work on her own, and we both agreed that she was ready for that. I suggested the empty chair technique. She put herself in one chair and her abusive father in the other chair. I recommended that she use a picture of her father or an object that represented him. From her chair, she started expressing all her feelings and thoughts toward her father without censoring her words. I wouldn't recommend this type of conversation with an abuser, as this could put you in danger, but in this imaginary therapeutic setting, it can often be beneficial. Reva expressed all her anger, sadness, grief, and confusion to her father. Then she sat in her father's chair and imagined how he would respond to her. She reported to me that her father's first words were about not taking responsibility and minimizing the abuse, but that didn't discourage Reva from expressing her deeper feelings as she switched back and forth between the two chairs. After an hour back and forth, Reva felt a sense of relief as the tension of her body melted away.

The empty chair technique also works for people who have experienced a secondary trauma. Secondary trauma can occur when someone is exposed to people who have been traumatized, disturbing descriptions of traumatic events, or people inflicting cruelty on others.[15] One of my clients, Laura, unsuccessfully attempted suicide after she was raped. When she was released from the hospital, she came to our treatment center. We worked with her and she was able to overcome her trauma. About a year later, her brother, Dan, called and requested treatment. He explained, "Seeing my sister go through the rape and then attempt suicide has traumatized me." I explained how secondary trauma like his was very normal and how we would work together to overcome it.

Dan had a lot of anger toward his sister for trying to commit suicide. He felt it was an extremely selfish thing to do and didn't understand how she could do that to him and the rest of the family. By utilizing the empty chair technique, we were able to work through this anger. During the session, we put an imaginary Laura in the empty chair while Dan sat across from her. I asked him to express his feelings to her directly. He could say anything he wanted to her, even though he might not ever say it in real life. He was given complete freedom to say what was on his mind.

He told her how upset he was for her putting him through the anguish of the suicide attempt. He told her he felt guilty for being angry at her. This went on for quite some time. I then requested that he switch chairs with his sister and get into her viewpoint. I

---

[15] R. Cieslak, K. Shoji, A. Douglas, E. Melville, A. Luszczynska, and C. C. Benight, "A Meta-analysis of the Relationship between Job Burnout and Secondary Traumatic Stress among Workers with Indirect Exposure to Trauma," *Psychological Services* 11, no. 1 (February 2014): 75–86, doi:10.1037/a0033798, accessed August 14, 2020.

told him to take a one minute of silence and then repeat what she had heard him say when he was in the other chair. The expression that came to his face told me that he was actually able to see what it was like to be in his sister's shoes. He went from anger to complete empathy. He truly felt the pain of his sister as a rape victim and had this beautiful dialogue back and forth, forgiving her. Through the empty chair technique, he was truly able to understand her feelings. As he shared his feelings of anger, he moved into sadness and eventually forgiveness. The process of forgiveness came about organically. I never told him he should forgive his sister.

Because he is now able to forgive her, he doesn't need to tell her this in person. Instead, he has been able to find inner peace about what happened. He may eventually want to talk to his sister about the experience, but it's not a requirement. This technique is great for allowing feelings to go deeper and deeper. You may try this without the help of a professional, but please make sure to stop if feelings become overwhelming.

## It's Okay to Feel Your Feelings

A lot of people try to get rid of feelings. Getting rid of them, as opposed to feeling and digesting them, is like cutting off a part of yourself. Imagine wanting to cut an arm or leg off your body. We are whole beings, and we have to experience ourselves as such. As noted previously, there is no such thing as a bad or good feeling—they are all okay. There is no such thing as a bad part of ourselves or a good part of ourselves. We have to accept every part of who we are. We cry because we're sad. We laugh because we're happy. We scream when we're scared. If you didn't feel anything, you would be like a robot. Every living being—including animals, plants, and trees—has feelings.

Accepting all your feelings is a vital lesson for children. If you're a parent, you are your children's role model. Let your children be sad and upset by allowing them to feel. Don't ignore them, but don't rush in to make them happy all the time. Don't make them scared of so-called negative feelings. When babies are born, they cry to communicate various things, such as hunger, tiredness, and fear. Crying is a survival tool—without it, a baby could die from hunger. Imagine if babies didn't cry. How would you know when to feed them? When to change wet diapers? Or whether they were sick or not?

What did your parents tell you about emotions? Do you remember how they treated you when you showed sadness or anger? Was that accepted? Did you notice a different reaction based on your gender or your siblings' gender? For example, some people believe that men aren't supposed to cry. Over the years, many clients have reported that "feelings were not welcome" in their households. They learned as children to portray a happy family to the outside world. Cultural influences may play a big role in how we deal with emotions as well.

## Exercise 11.2: Increase Your Tolerance to Feelings

1. Sit comfortably in a chair.
2. Put both feet on the floor, keep your spine erect and your eyes open, and notice your breathing.
3. Think of a recent happy incident or moment: walking on the beach with your best friend, playing with your dog, or going to an amusement park with your children.
4. Imagine being there and just notice your feelings. For the sake of this exercise, make sure they are positive feelings.

5. Notice where you feel the feelings in your body. In your heart? In your stomach? Feel the warmth of the happy feelings and expand this warmth throughout the body. Expand the feelings into your hands, feet, legs, face, and neck. Embody positive feelings.
6. After you stay in this state for a few minutes, think of a stressful situation or something that makes you feel sad.
7. Do a brief body scan to locate different sensations, such as tension. Where are you feeling sensations? What sensation gets your attention first? Stay with whatever is there. Notice the sensation and investigate it with curiosity and without judging. Just notice its rising and falling and shifting. If you get lost in thought, come back to your breath and again rest your attention on the body sensation. See if you can ride out the sensation like you would a wave in the ocean.
8. Keep focusing on the sensation for thirty seconds and then go back to the happy feeling again. Feel the expansion of the happy feeling in your body for a minute or so and then go back to the sad feeling for another forty-five seconds.
9. Go back and forth between the two feelings with the goal of increasing the time you spend on the sad feeling. Notice what happens when you go back and forth this way.

## Managing Stress through the HeartMath Technique

HeartMath, a stress management system founded by Doc Childre, helps you synchronize your brain and heart for optimal stress resistance. The core of the HeartMath philosophy is that the heart is the key to tapping into an intelligence that can provide us with fulfillment. Science has shown that the heart communicates with the body and brain on various levels. HeartMath offers exercises to help you connect to your heart and calm your nervous system. Here are some activities to try.

### HeartMath Breathing

Shift your attention to the area of your heart. As you slowly inhale and exhale, imagine your breath passing in and out through your heart area or the center of your chest. Breathe in an attitude of calm and balance. Breathe out an attitude of peace and serenity.

### Heart Lock-In

Rather than fixing something, Heart Lock-In is about experiencing your heart at a deeper level.

1. Shift your attention away from your head and focus on your heart.
2. Think of someone you love or care about. Feel the love in your heart. Focus on the feelings of appreciation and love. Try to stay with that feeling for five to fifteen minutes.
3. Gently send that feeling of love or appreciation to yourself and others.

### Freeze-Frame

This technique allows a major shift in perception. More than positive thinking, it creates a definitive, heartfelt shift.

1. Shift out of the head and focus on the area around your heart. Keep your attention there for at least ten seconds. Continue to breathe normally.

2. Recall a positive time or feeling and try to reexperience it. Try not to simply visualize it but rather to feel it in your heart. Stay in this position for at least a few minutes.
3. Ask a question from the heart: "What can I do in this situation to make it different?" or "What can I do to minimize stress?"
4. Listen to the response of your heart.

## Cut-Thru

Cut-Thru is a technique developed to help manage emotions. It gives you the ability to "cut through" complex, stuck emotions.

1. Be aware of how you feel about an issue or problem. Focus on your heart.
2. Assume objectivity. Act as though it were someone else's problem. What kind of advice would you give to a person who's just been slighted by a coworker? You'd probably say, "Hey, don't judge yourself. You are doing your best."
3. Take the distorted feelings and the emotions that are out of balance and bring them to the heart. Soak there in the heart, as if you were soaking in a warm bath. Practice letting the heart do the work for you.

In today's busy world, it seems that we are human doings, not human beings. It doesn't have to be that way. We need to center ourselves and stay in the present moment. Besides what I've outlined here, there are things you can do to connect to your heart. For centuries, people have been using meditation to reconnect. Martial arts is another practice that is all about discipline and being in the moment. While yoga is a physical activity like martial arts, it provides an opportunity to connect to yourself and your feelings. No matter how you choose to connect with yourself, your heart will greatly benefit.

## Ten Points to Remember

1. Accept all feelings as part of life.
2. Build gradual tolerance to feel your feelings.
3. Practice HeartMath.
4. Do joyful activities.
5. Follow your heart in making choices.
6. Choose friends who are committed to growing.
7. Know your strengths and weaknesses.
8. Connect to others.
9. Practice mindfulness.
10. Keep a daily journal of your feelings.

"Make your own Bible. Select and collect all the words and sentences that in all your readings have been to you like the blast of a trumpet."

—Ralph Waldo Emerson

# Step 5

# Reconnect to Spirituality, Community, and Nature

When something traumatic happens, it is devastating. Ralph Waldo Emerson's words encourage us to create our own spirituality. You may have noticed that all the previous steps (1–4) were about connecting to something inside of you. Step 5 is much different. It is about learning to connect to something much bigger than ourselves—spirituality, community, and nature.

CHAPTER 12

# When Trauma Happens, You Start to Question Your Beliefs

People often get confused about the difference between spirituality and religion. Consider spirituality more as a solitary experience of the divine. The English word *spirit* comes from the Latin *spiritus*, which means "breath." Although we often think of spirituality as something apart from our daily lives, it is as accessible as our next breath.[16]

Religion is more community driven, since it involves a group of people connected by their common faith or beliefs about the divine. Throughout time, religious and secular thinkers have formed communities of like-minded people. The original purpose of religion was to form a community. When something traumatic happens, we

---

[16] Manitoba Trauma Information and Education Centre, "Taking Care of Your Spiritual Self," MTIEC, 2013, https://trauma-recovery.ca/recovery/taking-care-of-your-spiritual-self/, accessed August 14, 2020.

often turn toward or away from what can provide us the most comfort. For example, when trauma happens to someone who is religious, they are either comforted by their religion or disconnected from it. They ask questions like:

- Why didn't God save me?
- Does God exist?
- Why didn't God protect me?

As a therapist, I don't have answers to these questions. I want to know about my client's belief system. A belief system is a set of principles or tenets that together form the basis of a religion, philosophy, or moral code. After clients share their belief systems with me, I can better understand where they are coming from.

A traumatic event can knock the breath out of you. No matter what your faith or spiritual belief, it can leave you feeling numb, distressed, and fully disconnected from that sense of something greater than yourself. How can we regain our spirituality and our deep connection to something bigger than us in difficult times?

Spirituality is a personal set of beliefs and experiences with many definitions. Spirituality is whatever you personally believe that gives you a sense of purpose in life and a sense of being part of something larger than yourself. It gives you a connection to the sacred. Most religions or spiritual systems talk about a higher being who knows all, who watches over and protects us.

Many children are hurt by the family members who are supposed to be their protectors. This is very confusing for a child, and it greatly impacts their faith in God or a higher being. If their own parents hurt them, why didn't God protect them? It is hard to understand how someone can be a victim of such an unfair situation. Why did God allow that? Why didn't God stop the abuse? You may have suffered at the hands of a religious group that misused religion and hurt you. You may find yourself questioning what to believe in. Can you relate to the following?

### Signs That You Are Disconnected from Your Spirituality

- Anger toward God
- Loss of faith
- Confusion
- Loss of purpose and meaning
- Isolation
- Making excuses not to reach out
- Overworking to avoid intimacy

Trauma affects a victim's spirituality and assumptions about life, and how meaning, purpose, and significance are derived beyond typical social or institutional structures. When your spirituality is disrupted, it shakes or can shatter your assumptions about life. You begin to question ideas about what is good, meaningful, or worthwhile. This explains why sometimes trauma victims suffer a crisis of faith—they feel God is responsible in some way for their trauma or they blame God for it. Often those who lose faith in God also lose faith in their religious community or their family and friends. As a result, they become isolated.

Existential questioning is a normal reaction to the experience of trauma. The search for meaning, for instance, generates great anxiety. If meaning isn't found, the result can be total despair and confusion.

Trauma generates other spiritual questions about the nature of God, the suffering of the innocent, and the relationship of God to creation. Trauma disrupts our ideas about ourselves. A traumatic event creates inner turmoil for victims. Coming to a resolution of the turmoil involves reintegrating the trauma, so that the inner self is able to find meaning and purpose. When people make sense of their trauma, they also find peace.

The experience of trauma may open the possibility for traumatized people to access their capacity for spiritual or religious coping. That is, they are capable of accessing spiritual resources that enable them to maintain well-being despite adverse circumstances. Their values and beliefs help them withstand the negative effects of trauma so they are able to bounce back quickly and resume normal functioning. Spirituality or religion contributes to resilience and the ability to cope with the negative effects of stress and trauma.

Trauma has the power to transform us and make us into more compassionate and caring individuals. In studies that examined the association between religious beliefs and trauma, the use of spirituality in therapeutic interventions proved beneficial for trauma victims. Trauma exposes the depths of the soul and may initiate a process of spiritual inquiry and soul-searching. It may serve as a "dark grace," leading one not to despair but to noble pursuits. For example, Saint Francis of Assisi's wartime experiences propelled him into a life of selfless service. Nelson Mandela turned his jail sentence into an opportunity to serve his country.

## Exercise 12.1: Your Belief System

Belief systems help inform everyday reality. They help us make sense of what happens to us, whether positive or negative. Answer the following questions and feel free to substitute the word Higher Power for God:

- While growing up, did you practice a particular religion? If so, which one?
- Do you believe in God? If so, what does your God look or act like?
- Do you believe in a God that is loving or punishing?
- What messages did your parents or guardians give you about God? Was the message that you will go to hell if you do something wrong, or was it that God is always there for you?

What we hear about God as a kid makes quite an impression on us. Have your belief systems changed as you've become an adult or do they remain the same?

---

## A Spiritual Bypass

Sometimes we use spirituality or religion to avoid our feelings. A spiritual bypass, according to John Welwood, is a "tendency to use spiritual ideas and practices to sidestep or avoid facing unresolved emotional issues, psychological wounds, and unfinished developmental tasks."[17] Welwood, a Buddhist teacher and psychotherapist, introduced the term in the early 1980s. Spiritual bypass is defined as the common use of one's spirituality, spiritual beliefs, spiritual practices, and spiritual life to avoid experiencing the emotional pain of working through psychological issues.[18] Recall

---

[17] Tina Fossella and John Welwood, "Human Nature, Buddha Nature: An Interview with John Welwood," *Tricycle: The Buddhist Review* 20, no 3 (2011).

[18] John Welwood, "Between Heaven and Earth: Principles of Inner Work," in *Toward a Psychology of Awakening* (Boston: Shambhala Publications, 2000).

that my client Yolanda wasn't allowed to grieve about her childhood abuse; her family wouldn't allow it because of their religious beliefs.

As part of a spiritual bypass, the victim of trauma is essentially saying, "I know what happened to me and I'm moving on. I forgive the people who hurt me and I forget what happened." Moving on without processing and digesting what truly happened is not healing. When you experience a traumatic event, belief systems get messed up and you may feel lost and lose your purpose. You lose who you are, don't know what you think, and can't feel your body. The pain is so great and the feelings are so overwhelming that you may zoom into the pain only and forget other parts of your life. That's how you can get frozen in the trauma. For instance, if you were abandoned by your parents, you might become hyper-focused on being abandoned. To properly heal from a traumatic experience, you need to integrate every part of you that was shattered during trauma. By doing so, you can reconnect to yourself. Healing from trauma opens your eyes to the greatness of life.

A few years ago I worked with a thirty-five-year-old woman, Renee, who was married with three children. She had been very active in her church community up until a few months before she came to see me. She often volunteered with children and felt very attached to the principles of the church. But faith alone didn't help her overcome her PTSD as her fellow churchgoers felt it should. She had frequent nightmares and flashbacks about childhood sexual abuse. They told her to pray harder and to forgive the perpetrators to find peace within. The more she shared her PTSD symptoms with others, the more she felt judged for not being "strong enough in her faith."

She felt like a bad person. While her ultimate goal was forgiveness, she couldn't skip grieving the trauma. My client had lost her childhood. Forgiveness is a choice. You don't have to forgive your perpetrator to heal trauma. That choice is up to you. But because her religious community was focused on only the forgiveness aspect, she wasn't able to express the hurt she felt.

She eventually abandoned the church and sought my professional help. At the end of her intensive treatment, her flashbacks and nightmares were completely gone. She said that what she got most out of treatment, however, was that she felt understood and not judged for the first time.

To make sense of what happened to you, it is helpful to talk to God to express your emotions. Sometimes the best way to do this is to create a spiritual pipeline straight to God.

## Exercise 12.2: Write a Letter to God

Write a letter to God just like you would write a letter to someone you know. Address it to whoever your God is: Creator of the Universe, Jesus, Allah, Buddha, or the Great Divine. Now, write your letter expressing your emotions. We are often told not to question God. Here is your opportunity to do so. After writing your letter, share it with your therapist or someone else you trust.

---

Speaking your words out loud can be powerful. After you've written your letter, you might want to share it with God by speaking it out loud. You can use the empty chair technique if you want.

## Exercise 12.3: Talking to God

Place two chairs across from each other. Sit down in one chair and consider the chair across from you to be God. Read your letter out loud to God. After sharing, if you are up to it, switch chairs and put yourself in God's shoes. Begin to have a dialogue with God as you switch back and forth between the chairs. Then answer the following questions:

- What was God's reaction to your letter?
- Do you see God in a different way now?
- What surprised you about this exercise?

---

No matter what your religious or spiritual beliefs are, being connected to a community is crucial in your healing. In the next chapter, I'll show you why community is so important and how to make community connections.

CHAPTER 13

# Why Community and Family Matter and How to Find Them

Having strong religious or spiritual faith helps those who have suffered abandonment, abuse, or neglect. Faith can bring people together and give you strength in dealing with hard days. Whatever you believe in, finding a group of like-minded people makes all the difference in your healing. Reach out to people you trust, connect with nature, explore your beliefs, pray, or meditate. You may find comfort in expressing your spirituality by exploring the tradition you were born into or by setting out to find a spiritual expression that fits who you are now—beginning with the firm knowledge that you are worthy of this quest. Your every breath is proof that you are already woven into the web of life.

## Reconnect to Your Loved Ones or Community

Trauma victims commonly isolate themselves due to shame and self-blame or to avoid hearing the wrong things said by loved ones. Many clients report feeling judged by others, and that is why they prefer isolation. They are often told, "Just move on. Your trauma happened when you were a child; you are a grown-up now" or "You don't want to get better. It's all in your head. You can overcome anything with your mind" or "Just get out of bed. I did it. You can too."

If you feel that no one understands your trauma, you will stop sharing. That's a pity, because one of the vital healing factors is the emotional support of others. Human beings are not supposed to be alone. In the Western Hemisphere, we often think that we must get through trials on our own.

As philosopher Jean Vanier said, "Community is a sign that love is possible in a materialistic world where people so often either ignore or fight each other." Often, your community might be yourself and just one other person. For example, after Keisha was raped, she immediately contacted her best friend. This friend accompanied Keisha to the police station and was there for Keisha whenever she needed her. She was able to talk about the incident and feel that sense of community support. As a result, she didn't develop trauma symptoms because the incident simply wasn't in her psyche anymore. She had the support of one, and that was all she needed to get better. Being isolated is the worst thing you can do.

While writing this book, I lost my beautiful residential Reconnect Integrative Trauma Treatment Center. It had been open for about eighteen months before the Woolsey Fire in California took it from me. The treatment center was an actual home built as a sanctuary for women who were suffering from trauma. On a Friday morning in November 2018, we were told to evacuate the home as the fire was approaching our area rapidly. Clients and staff packed some basic items and drove away to a safe area.

Exactly two days later, I got the devastating news that the center had completely burned to the ground. Shocked and grieving, I wasn't sure how to deal with this loss. Then something wonderful happened and helped me recognize the importance of community more than ever before. After the fire, I received more than 250 messages via Facebook, email, text, and phone from colleagues, clients, friends, and even family members from overseas. Each person extended sympathy and offered support. Never before had I experienced such a sense of group support. It kept me from feeling alone and gave me the strength to move forward. What does your community of support look like?

## Finding Your Tribe

Ideally, you want to reach out to people you trust and feel comfortable with. You want to find your tribe—a group that allows you to feel like you belong. Early on, your tribe might have been a sports team in school, the Boys & Girls Club, Girl Scouts, or Boy Scouts.

If you don't already have people in your life that you feel comfortable sharing with, support groups and group therapy are excellent options. If you have any addiction history, you may choose to join a recovery program, such as Alcoholics Anonymous (AA) or Smart Recovery. Twelve step groups like AA offer support in recovery and are there to help people struggling with addiction. The twelve step community offers an abundance of specific support groups, including those for overeating, gambling, love addiction, and sex addiction. The free meetings are an excellent way to meet people. Twelve step groups are not based on religion. Rather, they are based on the concept of a higher power, which provides a sense of connection to God. You can also join psychotherapy groups offered at many facilities across the country. The benefit of joining such a group is that you will be around others who are also working on their well-being, and this will make it easier for you to talk about your own emotional struggles.

However, *please* be careful about sharing and listening to other people's trauma stories. In my groups, I encourage participants not to get into details about their trauma because this can trigger other people who are not ready to hear it. It's not necessary to share details about what happened to feel the connection with another human being. A simpler approach is to talk about your *feelings* around the incident rather than the incident itself. If you feel your group puts too much focus on sharing the details of trauma, you may want to find another group.

The majority of my clients kept deep secrets of their traumatic history for years before they came to therapy. Having to keep secrets from others is very painful. It can also make you think that you did something wrong. If you were a sexual abuse victim, especially as a child, you may have been told by your perpetrator never to tell anyone because "no one will believe you anyway" or "I will hurt your family if you talk." Please know that there are many outstanding professionals who can offer a listening ear and a compassionate heart once you are willing to share your feelings. Although your past experience may make you believe that showing your vulnerability is dangerous, I want to encourage you as an adult to give it a try by reaching out to others.

## Seeking Comfort

As a therapist, I often hear victims describe the impact of trauma as having a "piece of my soul ripped out" or as having the spirit and body out of sync. Cultural practices and traditions serve many purposes. Often these traditions not only help define community but also create it. They also have healing qualities in that they help us make connections within ourselves, help us feel a sense of belonging, and strengthen a sense of identity and purpose. Exploring your own cultural heritage and practices can contribute to your recovery and well-being. So can learning about the traditions and practices of other cultures. We can borrow from other traditions if we find meaning, comfort, and connection in them. Curiosity and self-exploration are significant components of living well and being healthy.

There are many answers to the question of how we can live together. We need an open mind, a willingness to develop by our own standards, and a sturdy moral compass to find our way forward.

While post-trauma survival instincts may cause you to feel most comfortable trusting only yourself, isolating from others, or turning to coping behaviors such as drinking or working long hours, these behaviors may prevent you from reestablishing connection and trust in the world and yourself—and this is vital for healing from the effects of trauma and living a satisfying life. The effects of isolation can be even greater if you are living with the symptoms of PTSD caused by traumatic occurrences in childhood. In this case, you may never have had the chance to build or experience deep, loving relationships or trust in the world around you.

Once you have recognized these isolating behaviors as being the result of trauma, you have the choice to deliberately make decisions and take actions that can lead to connection and trust. This may feel frightening or difficult, and you may have thoughts about other people being unsafe, untrustworthy, or not worth the effort. It is important to take small steps that may seem counterintuitive to what your survival-based instincts are telling you. Then stop to reassess to see if your perceptions were true or not.

Group therapy and support groups can help you meet peers who may have experienced similar situations or symptoms, which can give you a chance to both talk to and hear from others who share similar struggles and triumphs. This can help you feel less alone in your experiences. In a group setting, you can learn valuable problem-solving ideas and skills. Support groups are often run for and by people who have had similar experiences, while group therapy run by one or more mental health professionals may involve directed therapeutic and relational interventions.

## Families

Although in general, family is defined as any group of people closely related by blood or marriage—such as parents, children, uncles, aunts, and cousins—we know very well that families can include much more than that. When you are born, you do not choose your family. But when you grow up, you have that option. If you are one of those lucky ones who have a good family and your trauma did not happen within that family, I strongly recommend that you reach out to family members as you are going through this healing journey. Isolation is a very common trauma symptom, and even though your family members may not know what to do with trauma, just having a relationship with them can help ease your pain. Also, educating family members about what trauma means and what trauma does can be highly beneficial. Right before

Reconnect clients graduate from our program, we meet with their family members and educate them about trauma. This helps clients normalize their experiences and helps with the healing process. You can also have a family member read this book to gain a better understanding of trauma.

If the trauma happened within your own family, this may not work for you. My client Kathy was sexually abused by her dad. She felt obliged to continue to have a relationship with him, as he was helping her financially. This is a very difficult situation and requires very strict boundaries to assure your safety and the safety of your kids, if you have them. For instance, Kathy would talk to her abusive father only if her husband was around and would never leave her two daughters alone with their grandpa.

You may also decide not to have a relationship with a family member who was abusive to you. Being related by blood should not make you feel obliged to have a relationship with them. As a child, you were not in control of many decisions. But now you have a right to choose whom you want to be around. This can sometimes cause a sense of guilt, which you can work on either by yourself or with the help of a therapist. Your safety and well-being should always be a priority. Either way, it is best to come up with boundaries that are right for you.

An alternative is to create your own family. Choose people you trust, such as friends, colleagues, or parents of friends, to be your extended family members. Because we are social animals, it is important to be connected to other humans, so go ahead and create your own tribe if your blood family has failed you.

CHAPTER 14

# Nature as a Healing Agent

Nature can help regulate our emotions. I didn't realize the importance of nature as a therapeutic tool until Maddie, a cult abuse survivor, became my client. Contrary to the way I grew up, she was raised in a rural environment, where animals and trees were her best friends. I met Maddie for the first time about four years ago. I remember walking to the waiting area to greet her. There I saw two young women sitting and chatting. I greeted them both and asked, "Which one of you is Maddie?" They both chuckled while Maddie responded with one word, "Me." I spent a minute or so chatting with both of them, trying to ease the nervousness I noticed Maddie was feeling.

She was dressed in jeans and a T-shirt, and her blond hair was in a ponytail. She was twenty-seven years old but appeared much younger. She had been referred to my trauma treatment center by her therapist, and we had talked on the phone about two weeks prior to our meeting. The therapist wanted Maddie to have intensive treatment with me for a couple of weeks, because she felt that once-a-week therapy was not sufficient to get Maddie out of her feelings of hopelessness and constant flashbacks.

Maddie seemed really uncomfortable at first, barely making eye contact with me. I tried to make her feel at ease, but I often got only one-word answers or head nods in response to my questions. There were many long silences. Maddie had signed up to do our program—six hours of therapy a day—for two weeks. I was to meet with her every day for two hours and help her process traumatic memories that were haunting her day and night. On our second day together, I noticed that sitting down and talking seemed torturous to her. Her body would almost shrink into the couch, and she would completely shut down and become mute. I worried whether I could really help her. I tried all the common tools and techniques I use with other clients—breathing and grounding exercises, visualizing a safe place, and tapping techniques—but with no result. In fact, the more techniques I tried, the more she retreated into the couch and became quiet. I had only two weeks to work with her, so I made the bold decision to throw away all traditional therapy methods and go for a walk with her. She smiled at my suggestion. I felt her relief.

Walking and being outdoors took all the pressure of "therapy" out of our therapeutic relationship. That's because you are both going forward in the same direction and you aren't staring at each other making eye contact. This was a good idea not only for her but for me as well. We started building rapport and trust through our walks. Maddie was able to talk when she moved her body, and I often paused her painful stories by bringing the trees or the warmth of the sun to her attention.

"How was last night? Were you able to sleep?" I asked her.

"No, not really. I had nightmares the whole night. I think it woke me up few times, but I am not sure."

"Is that common for you?"

"It is, unfortunately. I don't sleep much nights. I am really tired today and I feel nauseous also. I am getting fuzzy as I say this."

Maddie used the word *fuzzy* to describe how she felt when she was about to switch to one of her parts. You see, Maddie had been diagnosed a few years before meeting me with dissociative identity disorder (DID), formerly known as multiple personality disorder. She knew she had about fifteen parts, all different ages and genders. She often switched into a different part without even realizing it. When she came out of it, she would not remember what had happened.

To help ground her and prevent the switch from happening, I would say, "Look around and notice the trees. Feel your feet as we walk." I did this to make sure she didn't get overwhelmed with emotions. For Maddie, being out in nature was therapeutic. Through nature, we were able to work together each day to help her deal with her nightmares and flashbacks.

## What's Your Relationship with Nature?

Many adults loose the connection they had to nature when they were kids. How do we reconnect with nature? The good news is, it's easy to do and it's free. You simply step outside your door. When it comes to nature, use all your five senses: sight, smell, hearing, taste, and touch.

### Sight

Get outside and take a walk. Notice everything around you. Look up at the sky. Is it cloudy or a clear blue? What kind of beauty do you see in nature? What are the colors you see? Imagine you are a photographer and you've been tasked with taking ten unique photos outside in nature. What would you choose to take a photo of?

### Smell

Take in the smell after it's rained. Have you ever noticed the different smells of the different seasons? There is beauty in each season. There's nothing better than the smell of wet leaves in fall, the smell of pine trees in winter, the smell of dirt when planting flowers in spring, and the smell of fragrant flowers in summer. Did you know that plants and trees breathe in the carbon dioxide that we breathe out and use it to produce their own energy?

### Hearing

The sound of water flowing gently through a stream or the roar of the ocean at high tide can physically change your mind and body and help you relax.

### Taste

Enjoy the taste of fresh fruit and vegetables from your garden or someone else's garden. Farmer's markets are great options for buying fruits and vegetables in season. Not only is this a great way to connect with nature, but you can also eat healthier

### Touch

When was the last time you walked barefoot in the grass? I've shared how important grounding is. Walking barefoot is a great way to connect with Mother Earth and become aware of your surroundings. Time spent in the great outdoors is good for you. For years, researchers have been detailing how people who live near green spaces—parks, tree-lined streets, rural landscapes—have better physical and mental health than those without access to these spaces. Research has shown that barefoot contact with the earth can produce nearly instant changes in a variety of physiological measures, helping to improve sleep, reduce pain, decrease muscle tension, and lower stress.[19]

If you want to improve your well-being, embrace nature. Even just viewing nature pictures (such as landscape paintings and videos) can be therapeutic and reduce stress. Viewing natural beauty activates specific reward circuits in the brain associated with dopamine release, giving a sense of purpose, joy, and the energy to pursue your goals. Nature can be a pathway to human health and happiness. You can start embracing nature by simply going for a walk.

## Ten Points to Remember

1. Always be gentle with yourself.
2. Call friends and reach out for support.
3. Take care of your body and soul.
4. Surround yourself with supportive people.
5. Have or find spiritual or religious support.

---

[19] Washington Post, "Why Grounding—Walking Barefoot on Grass or Earth—Could Improve Your Health, from Better Sleep to Lower Stress, *Washington Post*, July 17, 2018, https://www.scmp.com/lifestyle/health-wellness/article/2155563/why-grounding-walking-barefoot-grass-or-earth-could, accessed August 14, 2020.

6. Spirituality doesn't have to involve an organized religion.
7. Your relationship with a higher power is a private relationship.
8. Remove yourself from people who are judgmental.
9. Respect the timing of your growth.
10. There is no right or wrong when it comes to spiritual beliefs and practices.

# Bonus Step

# Getting More Help

If you are struggling with flashbacks or vivid images of past events, or nightmares about being hurt, you might get relief by processing past memories related to these symptoms. Traumatic memories can get stuck, like a broken record at times, making it impossible for you to forget them.

Processing your trauma involves experiencing the trauma in an emotionally contained way. As trauma is stored both in the brain and body, retelling your story over and over again without the right supportive environment can create further stress. The goal of trauma therapy is to process the past while you stay connected to yourself in the present. Only after you build a capacity to stay present in the moment should you dive into the painful memories.

Know that although some of the processing can be done on your own, it is best to process traumatic memories with the help of an experienced trauma therapist. However, if you would like to process some of them on your own, one of the best ways to do it is through writing.

I strongly recommend that you do this step with the help of a qualified professional. However, if you have truly mastered the first five steps of this book and feel emotionally strong and ready to tackle the past memories, you may do it on your own.

CHAPTER 15

# Slow and Steady Wins the Race

Sometimes people talk about their memories as if they belonged to someone else. They talk about their memories without feeling anything, while being disconnected from themselves. The opposite also occurs: people become overwhelmed with their memories and emotions. When my client Olga shared memories of childhood sexual abuse, she would spend the following few days crying and unable to get out of bed. Prior to coming to see me, she had been to regular talk therapy and was told she had to tell her story over and over again until she felt better. The previous therapist had not helped Olga increase her tolerance for her emotions and memories by helping her stay grounded in her body.

When I told Olga that I would help her process the memories, at first she was terrified, and rightfully so. I assured her that I would prepare her carefully before working with the trauma story itself.

Trauma often creates negative beliefs, such as "I am bad" and "I am worthless." Creating a new meaning after trauma helps people move beyond such trauma-based beliefs. After building trust with Olga and helping her connect to her body and mind, we used techniques to process her memories. We worked very gently and slowly. I asked Olga to write down her feelings daily between our sessions and to practice the grounding techniques she learned in sessions.

I remember very clearly that during one of our sessions, after processing more details of her abuse, she burst into tears. This surprised me, as we had already talked about the most painful part of the memory without much tears. I asked her, "What brings the tears now?"

To that she responded, "It was not my fault." She continued, "I know logically that being abused is never a child's fault, but I could never let go of the guilt. And now as I was remembering how my cousin used to scare me and threaten me, I just felt like for the first time yelling back at him, 'It is not my fault! It is not my fault!'"

I asked her to sit with the feeling of letting go of the guilt and to allow every part of herself to really hear this and digest it. We sat in silence together for the next few moments as she continued to weep in relief.

Use your own judgment about whether you are ready to do the following exercise. Don't blame yourself if you aren't ready. That's okay. For this exercise to be beneficial, you need to make sure you can tolerate what will come up in terms of feelings or details of the memories. As you start writing about your past, you must stay in the present moment at the same time. If you cry, make sure you are not getting overwhelmed, holding your breath, feeling panicked, or hyperventilating. And if you start doing this exercise and feel your symptoms getting worse, please stop. It is best to have a support system around as you do the writing—someone who is nonjudgmental and caring so you can share your feelings with them just for emotional comfort. If you'd like, you can bring the exercise to your therapist and complete it with him or her.

## Exercise 15.1: Processing Memories

Make a list of what memories you would like to process. The list should be just headlines—with no details. Then rank the memories from the most painful to the least painful.

Starting with the least painful, write about the memory. But before you start writing, bring your attention to the here and now. Look around and remind yourself of the date and your present location. Evoke a sense of compassion in your heart. Think of someone you really love. Think of them when they are not feeling good and then tune into your heart. You may feel compassion for this person along with love. Hold that feeling and expand it throughout your heart and body. Stay with the feeling as you start writing down the memory.

It is crucial as you write that you stay as objective and as dispassionate as possible toward yourself. If you notice self-judgment coming up, pause and feel the compassion in your heart. Then continue to write from that angle.

As you write your memory, don't get stuck trying to remember the details. They are not as important as your feelings around the memory. If you feel no feelings, you may have become disconnected from yourself as a way to cope with the memory. Slow down, focus back on your heart, and try writing again.

Express all your feelings along with any sensations you may notice, such as smells, heat or cold, or bodily sensations. If you are crying a lot or your emotions feel overwhelming or unbearable, take a break. Don't push yourself. You can cause more damage if you push yourself beyond your limits. Don't judge yourself as weak or anything similar. Just pause, bring your attention to the here and now, and to the room where you are, and move around the room a little bit. If you feel like your nervous system is calming down, continue to write more memories. If not, try again another day.

End each writing by saying something positive to yourself: "I am sorry for what you have been through. It was not your fault. All of your thoughts and feelings are okay. You are okay and you are safe now. This was in the past." If you have a hard time saying these things to yourself, you may want to read an inspirational quote or poem, listen to an uplifting song, or call a friend.

The purpose of this work is to give your brain a new message: "Before, I was scared to talk about all this because it was not safe and I was not allowed to. Now it is okay. I can tolerate the feelings and memories, but I still will be very gentle with myself. It is now my decision."

After your first writing session, make an effort to observe yourself. How did you feel the rest of the day? How was your sleep? Do you remember any dreams or nightmares? Be honest with yourself to assess your capacity to tolerate this exercise. If you are feeling okay, you can either continue to write about the same memory or write about a second memory. If you are too overwhelmed, shorten the amount of writing time until you can build more tolerance for it.

---

When I feel that clients are emotionally strong enough, they can continue processing their memories and feelings by writing between sessions. An example is Steve, age forty-eight, who suffered from an attachment trauma when he was four years old. He was living in Russia at the time. When Steve's parents got divorced, his mom moved to another country. She was financially struggling and had to put Steve in a temporary home for about a month. Steve doesn't remember how he got there, but he remembers being left by his mom in a residential place for kids. He was alone, confused, and hungry. When he was younger, he used to call the place a "preschool"—a nice name he made up in order to deal effectively with the trauma of being left without his parents.

His mom put him there temporarily while she was looking for a place to live. He remembered pretending to be fine but feeling really sad inside. He reported to me that he had a sense of deep loneliness and a fear that logic couldn't explain. Although his physical well-being was not threatened, he felt like he was going to die. To deal with this fear and pain, he learned to disconnect from himself by going into a fantasy world in his thoughts.

The house didn't have enough food, and he was mostly fed dry bread and tea. He remembers starving and wanting to eat real food. He felt confused and abandoned. About a month later, his dad came to "rescue" him. His mom had given clear orders to the director of the house not to let his dad take him away. When his dad found him, he was very angry and had a fight with the director. She did not want Steve to go with his dad.

Steve and his father went to the home where he had lived with his parents. It was early evening and the table was set for dinner. He started eating like he had never eaten before. His father told him later that it was obvious he had gone hungry. As he watched Steve eat, he had tears rolling down his cheeks.

Steve and I worked on this hunger trauma during an eye movement desensitization and reprocessing (EMDR) session. EMDR is a therapeutic technique that uses rapid, rhythmic eye movements to process past traumatic events in a nontraditional way. During the session, Steve felt deeper emotions that he wanted to access on his own. During a quiet time at home, he started journaling about how he felt as a four-year-old. He was able to get deep into his emotions without getting too dysregulated. He truly got in touch with how he felt when he was little. He was able to connect with himself at that age. And with my guidance, he knew that while writing, he still had to feel his body and be aware of the current time, date, and place. As he got truly in touch with the fear of being hungry, he felt a deep sense of empathy toward that little Steve and made a step toward healing.

CHAPTER 16

# Different Types of Trauma Treatment

Many people who are looking for professional help from a therapist turn to Google for advice. I wanted to put myself in their shoes, so I went online and pretended to be someone who knew nothing about trauma and was searching for a treatment mode that could help me. One of the first items that showed up in my search was exposure therapy, which is a popular treatment for people with PTSD, especially military veterans. I was told what to expect in that first session:

- I would meet with a therapist.
- The therapist would record me telling my story during the session.
- I would go home and listen to the tape over and over again.
- I would return to therapy to share my experience.

To me, that sounds pretty scary. During a recent presentation to other therapists, I shared this story and asked them to imagine that they had been raped and had to listen to the story of this traumatic event over and over again. I then asked the audience, "Does anyone want to do that?" The response was an overwhelming no. There are some real risks here of retraumatizing yourself alone at home when you don't have the benefit of a trained therapist being with you. Most people would most likely not be able to tolerate listening to their story in their own voice over and over again. As a result, they might drop out and begin blaming themselves for being a "quitter." Coincidentally, exposure therapy has the highest dropout rate of all trauma treatment modalities.

## Common Reactions to Compromised Trauma Treatment

If you have any of the following reactions during or after therapy sessions, this might be a sign that you should slow things down:

- You are dissociating more than before treatment
- Your symptoms (flashbacks, nightmares, and so on) are worsening
- You quit therapy
- You are scared of trauma treatment
- You begin to self-injure or increase your self-harm behaviors

The most effective trauma treatment happens when you are able to ground yourself and calm your nervous system. You can do this without talking about the traumatic event itself. Throughout this book, I show you ways to do this.

## Is There a Right Way to Do Trauma Therapy?

Clinical psychologist Bessel van der Kolk attempts to integrate mind, brain, body, and social connections to understand and treat trauma. In his book *The Body Keeps the Score*, he discusses research showing how trauma reshapes both the body and brain, compromising sufferers' capacities for pleasure, engagement, self-control, and trust. He explores innovative treatments—from neurofeedback and meditation to sports, drama, and yoga—that offer new paths to recovery by activating the brain's natural neuroplasticity.

Like van der Kolk, we at Reconnect Treatment Center use an integrative approach that treats the whole person, creating a mind–body connection. Our integrative model utilizes the following modalities:

**Somatic experiencing,** developed by Peter Levine, is a body awareness approach based on the realization that human beings have an innate ability to overcome the effects of trauma by learning to release energy that has been stuck or frozen in the body. (See description of the fight, flight, or freeze response in chapter 3.)

- **Sensorimotor psychotherapy**, developed by Pat Ogden, is a body-based talk therapy that uses neuroscience to transform traumatic memories into strengths and resources.
- **Eye movement desensitization and reprocessing (EMDR)**, developed by Francine Shapiro, has become a powerful tool against trauma. EMDR works by unlocking the nervous system, allowing the brain to process and visualize disturbing material in a new, less distressing way. To date, EMDR has

helped an estimated half million people of all ages deal with many types of psychological distress.

- **Brainspotting,** developed by David Grand, is a powerful form of psychotherapy that can access parts of the brain often hidden from our awareness.
- **Emotional freedom technique** (EFT) is used instead of needles to stimulate the traditional Chinese acupuncture points. It can dramatically alleviate emotional disturbances along with many physical symptoms. It often works in minutes with commonly long-lasting results, and the side effects are almost always positive.
- **Mindfulness** involves cultivating an intentional awareness of the present moment. It can help people develop greater compassion toward others and less negativity, enhancing both relationships and health. It can be practiced at any time.
- **Yoga,** in all forms, can have profound therapeutic physical and psychological benefits. Through a deeper connection between mind and body, yoga produces anti-aging benefits by dramatically lowering stress, lifting mood, and helping you sleep better.
- **Medication** is sometimes used in addition to psychotherapy to treat trauma. Medication can especially help with traumatic symptoms such as depression, anxiety, eating disorders, and addictions. Consult a psychiatrist, not your general practitioner, to get evaluated for proper medication. Some people need medication and others don't.
- **Neurofeedback** is a form of training for your brain, promoting healthy function. It's like going to a gym for your brain. It can be an effective treatment alternative for those who do not respond well to medication.
- **Acupuncture** is a practice that dates back six thousand years. During this treatment, very thin needles are inserted

in the body to increase blood flow and to trigger the release of hormones such as endorphins and oxytocin. These hormones can relax the nervous system, lowering stress levels and anxiety. Acupuncture is also used to treat pain, headaches, digestive issues, and insomnia.

- **TRE**® is an innovative series of exercises that assist the body in releasing deep muscular patterns of stress, tension, and trauma.
- **Art therapy** uses the nonverbal language of art for personal growth, insight, and transformation, connecting thoughts, feelings, and perceptions with outer realities and life experiences. Researchers have discovered that traumatic experiences can become encoded in the mind in the form of images, almost like a camera taking a photograph. Making visual art is a unique way to express these traumatic images, bringing them to consciousness in a way that's less threatening than using words. The language of visual art—colors, shapes, lines, and images—speaks to us in ways that words cannot. Making art can help us express fear, anxiety, and other stressful emotions. You don't need to be an artist to express yourself in this form.
- **Music therapy** uses music to help facilitate physical, emotional, cognitive, and social change and growth. Qualified music therapists design interventions, including creating, performing, moving to, or listening to music, based on an individual's needs. Research shows that music helps us recognize and accept emotions, promotes self-expression and self-awareness, increases self-esteem, and facilitates relaxation and stress reduction.
- The **comprehensive resource model** (CRM) is a neurobiologically based trauma treatment program created by Lisa Schwarz that uses breathing techniques and grounding

skills. It creates a bridge between the most primitive aspects of a person's brain and the purest, healthiest part of the self. This process takes a person from feeling lost and insignificant to embracing who they are. The goal is to bring their brain and body into a state of neurobiological safety as they learn to tolerate intolerable memories thereby releasing frozen behavior and thinking patterns.

CHAPTER 17

# How to Choose a Therapist

The history of trauma treatment has progressed—from a time when symptoms were associated with cowardice to the present-day approach, whereby symptoms are recognized by mental health professionals and treated through therapy. Many people believe traditional modalities such as cognitive behavioral therapy (CBT) and exposure therapy are the best ways to treat trauma. CBT, a form of talk therapy, aims to change the patterns of thinking or behavior that are behind people's difficulties. Exposure therapy exposes patients to the causes of their anxiety without any accompanying harm. The process is intended to help people overcome anxiety or distress.

Because trauma is so prevalent, trauma treatment has become very popular. But many therapists are doing trauma work with their clients in hurtful ways. Often, people are looking for a quick fix or a shortcut rather than a long-term solution. Shaman-led groups, psychedelic drug-controlled therapies, deep breath work, past life therapies, dysregulating experiential group therapy, and other "enlightening" approaches have become popular.

At Reconnect, we believe in working on trauma in a slow, gentle way. This is truly a journey that takes time. Strong cathartic experiences such as heavy crying or profound, mind-blowing insights are not necessary. You are more likely to keep the benefits long term if you gradually heal your past trauma by working on memories slowly instead of doing intense, ten-hour drug-induced therapy.

Today we know the importance of incorporating the body into trauma treatment. However, be careful with therapy that encourages you to leave your body; it may have side effects, such as dissociation or being overly dependent on your therapist.

## What to Look for in a Therapist

When seeking a qualified therapist, look for someone who does body-based therapy and has been trained to treat trauma in one of the previously mentioned modalities.

When choosing a therapist, consider the process to be a job interview—they interview you and you interview them to determine if it's a good fit. Ask the following questions and note the preferred answers.

## Questions to Ask

1. Do you believe I have to be able to talk about my trauma in order to heal? **A:** No, it's not necessary.
2. Are you trained in any body-based therapy? **A:** Yes.

3. Do you have experience treating clients who have trauma? **A:** Yes.
4. What treatment models did you study? **A:** EMDR, Brainspotting, somatic treatment modality, and mindfulness.
5. Do you use exposure treatment for trauma therapy? **A:** No.
6. Do you use hypnosis for trauma therapy? **A:** No.
7. Can you treat me even if I don't have memories of my trauma? Do you believe I should eventually remember everything? **A:** Yes, I can treat you. And no, you don't have to remember exactly what happened.
8. What is your philosophy about trauma treatment in general? **A:** I believe in a client-centered and gentle treatment. I don't believe in pushing the client into doing something they don't want to do.

Because we often don't recognize trauma in our lives, the idea of seeking professional help to deal with trauma often feels unnecessary. We simply learn to cope with trauma until it becomes overwhelming. The main reason people don't seek treatment is that they are scared about what will happen as a result of disclosing their trauma in an honest, authentic way. They don't want to relive something traumatic, especially in front of a stranger.

## Ten Points to Remember

1. Know what trauma is and the impact it had on you.
2. Don't judge your symptoms.
3. Be aware of how you talk to yourself at all times.
4. Don't talk about traumatic memories without first spending time on building your resources.

5. Don't rush the process.
6. Ask for the support of others.
7. Remember that trauma healing is a journey, not a race.
8. Go with what is right for you and not for someone else.
9. Surround yourself with the right people.
10. Stay in the present time and don't go into the future or the past with your thoughts.

CHAPTER 18

# Wrapping Up

I cannot emphasize enough how important it is to stay in the present. And I'm not talking about doing this just when dealing with trauma. Staying in the present is helpful for stress management and ongoing well-being. In the 2001 book *The Power of Now*, Eckhart Tolle shared that the key to finding inner peace is leaving your analytical mind and ego behind as you tap into the now—which is in the body, the silence, and the space all around you. This book is considered a classic, has sold more than five million copies worldwide, and has been translated into thirty languages, so obviously people relate to the concept and understand it, but many of them don't put it into practice. This is a pity. Being in the present moment is one easy thing you can do to reconnect to yourself. Practice makes perfect. Psychologists used to say that it takes twenty-one days to form a new habit. But a 2009 study by University College London researchers concluded that, on average, it takes sixty-six days for a new behavior to become automatic.[20]

As you embark on this healing journey, remember the five steps to reconnecting:

### Step 1: Understand Trauma

To understand yourself and to normalize your feelings, you need to know what trauma is. During this step, you discover what trauma does to your physical and emotional well-being.

### Step 2: Reconnect to Your Mind

During and after a traumatic event, your brain shuts down and makes it very difficult for you to think straight and make decisions. After you understand what trauma is and some of your reactions to it, you can start thinking clearly again and make decisions that benefit your well-being. Trauma clouds the way you think. Use mindfulness techniques to get clear minded and reconnect with your mind.

### Step 3: Reconnect to Your Body

Trauma may have disconnected you from your body through dissociation. In this step, you use practical exercises and methods to reconnect to your body.

---

[20] Healthline, "How Long Does It Take for a New Behavior to Become Automatic?" Healthline, 2020, https://www.healthline.com/health/how-long-does-it-take-to-form-a-habit#the-21-day-myth, accessed August 14, 2020.

### Step 4: Reconnect to Your Heart and Emotions

This step allows you to recognize how being disconnected from your feelings and not dealing with negative feelings can repress your emotions. This step allows you to gradually feel those repressed emotions and reconnect with your heart and emotions through guided exercises.

### Step 5: Reconnect to Spirituality, Community, Nature, and Family

In this step, you learn how you may have isolated yourself due to trauma. You recognize the dangers of isolation and the benefits of support from others. You examine how trauma has created a core disconnect from your faith—whether that's from God, spirituality, or a connection with nature and the universe—and you restore that connection.

Keep up these practices each and every day. By doing so, you'll find more freedom from the trauma. This book isn't intended to be something you read and then put on your bookshelf to collect dust. It is to be incorporated into your life each and every day.

If I told you there is *one* thing you can do to be happy for the rest of your life, would you do it? And if I told you that you need to do it daily, would you do it? Most people respond with a resounding yes. What's is that one thing?

Stay grounded in your body and stay focused on the present at all times.

Here's the problem with not being present at all times: We start negotiating with ourselves. I do this myself. I say, "I'm going to stay present 80 percent of the time." I realize that this is stinking thinking, because in that remaining 20 percent time period, something stressful can happen. I can slip into the past and begin worrying about the future. The next thing I know, I've spent the whole day worrying about the future. It's a slippery slope.

I want to be clear. This doesn't mean you can't plan for the future and set goals for what you want to achieve. Here's a simple example: If I'm thinking about what I'm going to make for dinner tomorrow, I can still be present as I notice my hands are wet while I'm washing the dishes or my feet are touching the ground as I'm sitting in a comfortable chair. I'm still very present in the moment.

I encourage you to reread each of the ten points at the conclusion of each of the five parts of this book to stay on track. What will you do to stay in the present moment to help yourself reconnect? If you feel like therapy might be something you'd like to pursue, I encourage you to read the sections that detail what types of therapies are available and how to find a good therapist.

# About the Author

Dr. Karol Darsa is a licensed psychologist and the founder and executive director of Reconnect Integrative Trauma Treatment Center, which she established in Los Angeles in 2014. This one-of-a-kind treatment center integrates all evidenced-based cutting-edge trauma treatment modalities under one roof. A survivor of childhood trauma, she understands the challenges and joys of the journey of healing.

Dr. Darsa co-created the Invisible War Recovery Program, an intensive trauma treatment program for veterans suffering from military sexual trauma. The producers sought out Dr. Darsa to create this special program for the featured veterans due to her extensive experience and proven methods of working with trauma. The program was inspired by the Academy Award-nominated documentary "The Invisible War."

She has been interviewed by Katie Couric, Susan Ortolano, and Lisa Tahir, and was featured on the Voice of America. She lectures about trauma treatment at various universities such as the University of Southern California, UCLA and Cal Lutheran. She also speaks at treatment centers and conferences.

Dr. Darsa began her career in 1998 as a foster care social worker. She studied evidence-based trauma treatment techniques and established herself as a trauma specialist. Her goal is to help clients release and heal from their trauma without becoming overwhelmed, using an approach that is gentle but direct. Dealing with the effects of trauma and traumatic memories takes time, so she encourages clients to work at their own individualized pace and to trust in their innate ability to heal.

Reconnect Integrative Trauma Treatment Center:
https://www.reconnectcenter.com/

Facebook: https://www.facebook.com/Reconnect-Integrative-Trauma-Treatment-Center-281697125367884/

LinkedIn: https://www.linkedin.com/in/karol-darsa-22300583/

To book Dr. Karol Darsa to speak, please fill out the inquiry form on the webpage below:

https://www.reconnectcenter.com/contact/

# Letter to the Readers

Dear Reader.

First of all, I want to thank you for reading *The Trauma Map*. It took me quite a long time to make the decision to write a book, however, once started, I experienced the joy of knowing that I could be a guide in someone else's growth or healing. And, I decided to write it even if it meant you're the only person I helped.

There is no greater joy than being the support system helping someone else experience their life fully and without trauma. Being able to really help someone feel better was at the root of my decision to become a therapist to begin with. *The Trauma Map* is another extension of that desire. I have always wanted to serve other people— to help them change their lives. It has been important to me to reach out with this book, especially to those who can't afford therapy.

Over the years I have seen so many people impacted by traumas big and small. I have also witnessed thousands who have had neither the chance to eliminate their trauma by getting treatment nor the opportunity to work through it. That is why my biggest passion is to educate others about what trauma means, how it impacts one's life, and how to give them hope so they know there really is a chance to come out of it.

I hope you got more than you expected out of this book and, if so inspired, that you share it with others. For more information on workshops for self-development focused on trauma healing, or to join my mailing list, connect through my website. If you're ever in the Los Angeles area, you have a standing invitation to visit our treatment center.

In gratitude,

Dr. Karol Darsa

ReconnectCenter.com
drdarsa@reconnectcenter.com

# Acknowledgments

I would like to express my special thanks and sincere gratitude to my teacher and mentor, Christine Schenk, who, over the past 18 years of my study, has been the most crucial person in my own healing. The invaluable guidance Christine provided through my personal journey paved the way for me to help hundreds of others heal their own traumas.

I want to acknowledge my children, Tal and Gil, for their patience as I stole time away from them to focus on the book. To my ex-husband, Oded, for supporting me as a co-parent, enabling me to productively use the countless hours I spent away from my children.

I extend my heartfelt thanks to my family in Turkey and Spain who have always shown such a deep level of encouragement and support throughout this wonderful project.

I cannot express enough thanks to my talented staff at Reconnect Trauma Treatment Center for their trust, communication, and understanding by helping the hundreds of people who came through our doors. And my right hands — yes, there are two — Shilloy Sanchez and Jorge Rivera. It was a great comfort to know you provided the management needed in the running of Reconnect, giving me the time to write this book.

My journey started several years ago with coaching from Maia Akiva. Her inspirational, fun activities, and knowledgeable eye got me incredibly excited about writing and started me down the author's path.

My completion of this project could not have been accomplished without the knowledge and patience of my editor, Corrine Casanova, who helped me to edit, re-edit, and re-edit again. Of course, I want to give special thanks to Daily House Publishing, especially to Kitty Turner, whose help created a vibrant, exciting, and thorough publishing and marketing roadmap.

I want to thank the talented artist, Tim Johnson, for the drawing of this beautiful tree. Not only has it been the inspiration for the cover of my book, the fact that it hangs in my living room is a daily reminder of the deep roots of grounding and strength.

I am extremely grateful to Babette Rothschild, who has been a friend and a mentor to me in organizing my thoughts and is someone I highly admire as an author and as a psychotherapist. I cannot thank you enough for our lunches and your honest and direct feedback.

Finally, to the following friends for supporting me in their own uniquely different ways: Seth Kadish, Kelly McDaniel, Andy Lorenzo, Tuba Guvelioglu, and Polet Abut. Their ideas, feedback, and always encouraging words have earned my deepest appreciation.

# Recommended Reading

Cameron, Julia. *The Artist's Way: A Spiritual Path to Higher Creativity.* NY: Penguin/Random House, 1992.

Levine, Peter. *Healing Trauma: A Pioneering Program for Restoring the Wisdom of Your Body.* Louisville, CO: Sounds True, 2008.

———. *Waking the Tiger: Healing Trauma,* NY: North Atlantic Books, 1997.

McDaniel, Kelly. *Ready to Heal: Breaking free of Addictive Relationships.* Carefree, AZ: Gentle Path Press, 2012.

Mountrose, Philip, and Jane Mountrose. *The Heart and Soul of EFT and Beyond: A Soulful Exploration of Emotional Freedom Techniques and Holistic Healing.* North Wahroonga, Australia: Holistic Communications, 2006.

Muller, Wayne. *Legacy of the Heart: The Spiritual Advantages of a Painful Childhood,* NY: Touchstone, 1993.

Rothschild, Babette. *Eight Keys to Safe Trauma Recovery: Take-Charge Strategies to Empower Your Healing.* NY: W. W. Norton, 2010.

Tolle, Eckhart. *The Power of Now: A Guide to Spiritual Enlightenment.* Novato, CA: New World Library, 2004.

Van der Kolk, Bessel. *The Body Keeps the Score: Brain, Mind, and Body in the Healing of Trauma,* NY: Penguin Books, 2015.

APPENDIX

# Quizzes and Exercises

The following exercises were referred to in chapter 2.

## Life Events Checklist[21]

Throughout our lives, we may experience things that we don't consider traumatic, but they leave an impact on us. The following are stressful things that sometimes happen to people. For each event, check one or more of the boxes to the right to indicate that: (a) it happened to you personally, (b) you witnessed it happen to someone else, (c) you learned about it happening to someone close to you, (d) you're not sure if it fits, or (e) it doesn't apply to you. Be sure to consider your entire life (childhood and adulthood) as you go through the list of events.

[21] U.S. Department of Veterans Affairs, "PTSD: National Center for PTSD," U.S. Department of Veterans Affairs, July 2, 2020, http://www.ptsd.va.gov, accessed September 2, 2020.

| Event | Happened to me | Witnessed it | Learned about it | Not sure | Doesn't apply |
|---|---|---|---|---|---|
| 1. Natural disaster (e.g., flood, hurricane, tornado, earthquake) | | | | | |
| 2. Fire or explosion | | | | | |
| 3. Transportation accident (e.g., car, boat, train, or plane crash) | | | | | |
| 4. Serious accident at work, home, or during a recreational activity | | | | | |
| 5. Exposure to toxic substance (e.g., dangerous chemicals, radiation) | | | | | |
| 6. Physical assault (e.g., being attacked, hit, slapped, kicked, or beaten up) | | | | | |

| Event | Happened to me | Witnessed it | Learned about it | Not sure | Doesn't apply |
|---|---|---|---|---|---|
| 7. Assault with a weapon (e.g., being shot, stabbed, or threatened with a knife, gun, or bomb) | | | | | |
| 8. Sexual assault (e.g., attempted rape, forced to perform any type of sexual act) | | | | | |
| 9. Other unwanted or uncomfortable sexual experience | | | | | |
| 10. Combat or exposure to a war zone (in the military or as a civilian) | | | | | |
| 11. Captivity (e.g., being kidnapped, abducted, held hostage, or taken prisoner of war) | | | | | |

| Event | Happened to me | Witnessed it | Learned about it | Not sure | Doesn't apply |
|---|---|---|---|---|---|
| 12. Life-threatening illness or injury | | | | | |
| 13. Severe human suffering | | | | | |
| 14. Sudden, violent death (e.g., homicide, suicide) | | | | | |
| 15. Sudden, unexpected death of someone close to you | | | | | |
| 16. Serious injury, harm, or death you caused to someone else | | | | | |
| 17. Any other very stressful event or experience | | | | | |

There is no formal scoring protocol. This checklist simply provides information about what traumatic experiences you've gone through.

## What's Your ACE Score?

Your ACE score can help you determine your risk factors for PTSD. The ACE Study measured ten types of childhood trauma. Five are personal: physical abuse, verbal abuse, sexual abuse, physical neglect, and emotional neglect. Five are related to other family members: a parent who's an alcoholic, a mother who's a victim of domestic violence, a family member in jail, a family member diagnosed with a mental illness, and the disappearance of a parent through divorce, death, or abandonment.

There are many other types of childhood trauma, including experiencing racism, being bullied, watching a sibling being abused, losing a caregiver, experiencing homelessness, surviving and recovering from a severe accident, witnessing a father being abused by a mother, witnessing a grandmother abusing a father, involvement with the foster care system, and involvement with the juvenile justice system. These ten childhood traumas were the focus of the ACE Study because they were mentioned as most common by a group of about three hundred Kaiser health insurance members. These traumas have also been well studied individually in the research literature.

The ACE score is meant as a guideline. If you experienced other types of toxic stress over months or years, those will likely increase your risk of health consequences.

To determine you score, answer the following questions.

Prior to your eighteenth birthday:

1. Did a parent or other adult in the household often or very often swear at you, insult you, put you down, humiliate you, or act in a way that made you afraid that you might be physically hurt?
   ____ No
   ____Yes

2. Did a parent or other adult in the household often or very often push, grab, slap, or throw something at you, or hit you so hard that you had marks or were injured?
   ____ No
   ____Yes

3. Did an adult or person at least five years older than you ever touch or fondle you or have you touch their body in a sexual way? Did they attempt to or actually have oral, anal, or vaginal intercourse with you?
   ____ No
   ____Yes

4. Did you often or very often feel that no one in your family loved you or thought you were important or special? Did you feel that your family members didn't look out for each other, feel close to each other, or support each other?
   ____ No
   ____Yes

5. Did you often or very often feel that you didn't have enough to eat, had to wear dirty clothes, or had no one to protect you?

Were your parents sometimes too drunk or high to take care of you or take you to the doctor if you needed it?
_____ No
_____Yes

6. Were your parents ever separated or divorced?
_____ No
_____Yes

7. Was your mother or stepmother often or very often pushed, grabbed, or slapped? Did she have something thrown at her? Was she sometimes, often, or very often kicked, bitten, hit with a fist, or hit with something hard? Was she ever repeatedly hit for a few minutes or threatened with a gun or knife?
_____ No
_____Yes

8. Did you live with anyone who was a problem drinker or alcoholic, or who used street drugs?
_____ No
_____Yes

9. Was a household member depressed or mentally ill? Did a household member attempt suicide?
_____ No
_____Yes

10. Did a household member go to prison?
_____ No
_____Yes

Add up your "yes" answers. This is your ACE score.

## Abbreviated PCL-C

The following questions concern problems and complaints that people might have in response to stressful life experiences. Indicate how much you have been bothered by each problem in the past month by circling the number that corresponds with "not at all," "a little bit," "moderately," "quite a bit," or "extremely."

| | | **Not at all** | **A little bit** | **Mod-erately** | **Quite a bit** | **Extremely** |
|---|---|---|---|---|---|---|
| **PCL1** | Repeated, disturbing memories, thoughts, or images of a stressful experience from the past? | 1 | 2 | 3 | 4 | 5 |
| **PCL2** | Repeated, disturbing dreams of a stressful experience from the past? | 1 | 2 | 3 | 4 | 5 |
| **PCL3** | Suddenly acting or feeling as if a stressful experience from the past were happening again (as if you were reliving it)? | 1 | 2 | 3 | 4 | 5 |

| | | Not at all | A little bit | Mod-erately | Quite a bit | Extremely |
|---|---|---|---|---|---|---|
| **PCL4** | Feeling very upset when something reminded you of a stressful experience from the past? | 1 | 2 | 3 | 4 | 5 |
| **PCL5** | Having physical reactions (e.g., heart pounding, trouble breathing, sweating) when something reminded you of a stressful experience from the past? | 1 | 2 | 3 | 4 | 5 |
| **PCL6** | Avoiding thinking or talking about a stressful experience from the past or avoiding having feelings related to it? | 1 | 2 | 3 | 4 | 5 |

| | | Not at all | A little bit | Mod-erately | Quite a bit | Extremely |
|---|---|---|---|---|---|---|
| **PCL7** | Avoiding activities or situations because they reminded you of a stressful experience from the past? | 1 | 2 | 3 | 4 | 5 |
| **PCL8** | Having trouble remembering important parts of a stressful experience from the past? | 1 | 2 | 3 | 4 | 5 |
| **PCL9** | Loss of interest in activities that you used to enjoy? | 1 | 2 | 3 | 4 | 5 |
| **PCL10** | Feeling distant or cut off from other people? | 1 | 2 | 3 | 4 | 5 |
| **PCL11** | Feeling emotionally numb or being unable to have loving feelings for those close to you? | 1 | 2 | 3 | 4 | 5 |

| | | Not at all | A little bit | Mod-erately | Quite a bit | Extremely |
|---|---|---|---|---|---|---|
| **PCL12** | Feeling as if your future somehow will be cut short? | 1 | 2 | 3 | 4 | 5 |
| **PCL13** | Having trouble falling or staying asleep? | 1 | 2 | 3 | 4 | 5 |
| **PCL14** | Feeling irritable or having angry outbursts? | 1 | 2 | 3 | 4 | 5 |
| **PCL15** | Difficulty concentrating? | 1 | 2 | 3 | 4 | 5 |
| **PCL16** | Being super alert or watchful or on guard? | 1 | 2 | 3 | 4 | 5 |
| **PCL17** | Feeling jumpy or easily startled? | 1 | 2 | 3 | 4 | 5 |